to be known

to be known

WHEN HURT FINDS HEALING AND IDENTITY IS REWRITTEN

MICHELLE RABY

R M Davis

MICHELLE RABY
SACRAMENTO

R M Davis – Contributing Writer

Sarah Nelson Katzenberger – Editor

Staci Stewart – Editor

Christa Sibbett- Editor

Renee Ross – Editor

Joseph Raby – Book Layout and Design

Trent Ellerman – Cover Design

Dedication

To my Joe Joe, Cohen Boy, and Sweet Annalee...I
love you with all my heart!

Contents

Preface

There is one truth that is consistent in life—we all have a story. Our past experiences collaborate to shape and define the emotional and spiritual facets of ourselves that ultimately dictate our life's journey and destination. The past has incredible power. It can influence our reactions and responses, our beliefs and perceptions, and more importantly, determine our present and future.

There is another truth that is consistent in life, but rarely understood or accepted. It is this: God can redefine a person's present and future, despite the shadows of their past. Their story's theme can, without question, be rewritten by allowing God to place new ink on the pages. I make this statement and write this book with absolute assuredness, because I am a testament of a life's story redefined by God Himself.

As you read ahead, you will see based on my upbringing and history that my life could have had a much different ending. Rather than joy, there could have been great sorrow. Rather than hope, there could have been despair. Hardship was poised to define my future, but rather than succumb to the inevitable, I came to experience and accept the undeniable:

God's promise to be unwavering and unchanging on my behalf, and to bring unmeasured peace and joy into my life. With my hand in His I can expect Him to do abundantly more than I ask or think, and to outdo Himself today, tomorrow, and always. From an early age my value and significance was in jeopardy of being erased, but a lovingly God had other plans.

For some, a promise of renewal might be too good to be true. Perhaps that person is you. But I challenge you as you read my story to accept that God truly desires to redefine lives and transform stories of sadness and shame. Then, once this truth settles in your heart, begin to expect that through the healing of wounds and infusion of hope, God will faithfully pen new chapters that will reveal all He has waiting for you.

PART I

The Future

"Never be afraid to trust an unknown future to a known God."

~ Corrie ten Boom

1

In His Hands

It was a Thursday night in May. Joe and I were sitting on the couch watching a movie, attempting to follow the plot in between contractions. As first-time parents we curiously looked at each other after the pains subsided, hoping the other would know if it was time to be concerned. Since the intervals hadn't changed much, still about ten minutes apart, and the pains hadn't intensified significantly, I decided to go to bed, hoping a change in position would relieve the pain in my back.

I dozed off for a bit. Then, whoa! I was fully alert! That pain felt much different than it had over the past few hours. I glanced at the clock to make a mental note.

11:00 p.m.

Joe had finally drifted off so I decided not to wake him — not right then at least. I shifted my position and adjusted the pillow hoping it would help relieve the pressure. Now wide-awake, I listened intently to the clock as it ticked down the moments to the most amazing adventure of my life.

I was going to be a mom soon.

Quite possibly, in a matter of hours I would be meeting my baby boy, my son, in person for the first time.

Responding to a sudden flutter and roll in my stomach, I gave a gentle pat to acknowledge my son's acrobatics. I opened my eyes and watched my husband as he slept. I knew Joe would be an amazing father. No human being, no person in my life, has ever loved me like Joe. I often say it is the closest thing to God's love that I have ever experienced. And I knew he would love our son just as deeply and completely as he loves me.

As I thought of the two of them together, my heart filled with immense joy. It was as if the emotion was rushing through floodgates — mighty, powerful, unstoppable joy. I was convinced no heart was made to hold so much happiness, yet God continued to bless me beyond measure. Overwhelmed, I had to catch my breath. Tears welled in my eyes as I realized this *must* be God's promise of joy unspeakable.

Joe turned onto his side and cleared his throat. It made me smile because it sounded a bit like the engine sounds he makes when he reads *Cars and Trucks and Things That Go* to the baby. We decided early in the pregnancy that we would read to the baby every night we could — for all the reasons you'd expect, and one you wouldn't.

First and foremost, we wanted to establish a bond with the baby. We wanted the sound of our voices to be familiar and soothing to him. Much like God wants His children to recognize and know His voice, we wanted our son to identify with and trust our voices as early as possible.

Second, believing that babies respond to stimuli while in the womb, we wanted to give our son a strong foundation for intellectual and spiritual development, as well as ignite character, vision, and passion in his innocent and receptive heart.

Our nightly reading adventures would accomplish one more very significant thing. It would give me an opportunity to read — better. It was a secret I had always protected, but the truth was I struggled with reading. A foundation for learning was not afforded to me at an early age. The instability and chaos that defined my life simply overshadowed the need. Unfortunately, the effects followed me throughout adulthood, making books a challenge. But now things were about to change. "Mom" was going to be my name, and I felt a strong desire and determination to give my son all that I had missed. Struggle and shame would not be his road, and I would make any investment necessary to ensure his future did not mirror my past.

So at Joe's suggestion we began to read aloud to our son. Joe's parents had sent us some of the books Joe read as a child — *Berenstain Bears* and *Children's Bible Books*, to name a few. When we first received them it was fun to see the delight in Joe's eyes as he reminisced about reading the stories, and I imagined one day our son would share similar memories with his children, too. As we established our reading ritual, it was humbling at first, Mom learning along with the baby.

But the kindness and consideration Joe provided throughout the process gave me a safe place to be vulnerable. His gentle encouragement to sound out the words and his affirmation that I was doing fine gave me the courage to tackle the challenges necessary to become the parent I wanted to be — the parent I had wished for as a little girl.

When the next contraction subsided, I nudged Joe with the possibility that this might be it, and we quickly prepared for the long-anticipated trip to the hospital. Joe grabbed my bag as I put on my robe and walked gingerly down the hall past the baby's room. For weeks we had worked diligently on the nursery. While the hope of most expectant mothers is that they "did it right," my hope was that I "didn't do it wrong."

Throughout our preparations, simple decisions proved challenging because the fear of "not getting it right" constantly nagged at me. Like the day I stood in front of the dresser not having a clue which drawer should hold the diapers. As I stood there frustrated and embarrassed, Joe very sweetly assured me there was no wrong place.

But how would I know that? How would I know the right way to prepare for a child, to nurture a child? How could I know what a mom was, when I hadn't experienced what a mom should be? All I was sure of, was that I wanted my son to feel the love that went into his room. My only prayer could be that I adequately expressed a love I had never experienced from my mother.

After the doctor's examination at the hospital, it was determined our son was not yet ready to meet us, so we returned home at 4:30 in the morning.

Tired and weary I whispered an invitation to our boy, "Come out and play, Cohen William."

Saying his name out loud reminded me of how important the name selection process had been. Because we wanted him to grow in the knowledge and wisdom of God, and to serve our Heavenly Father with unwavering faith, we chose the name Cohen, meaning "priest." His middle name, William, was after his Paw-Paw and meant "protector." Growing up, I struggled with my identity. I never had a firm grasp of who I was or who I was meant to be. It was imperative to me that my child have a clear understanding of his worth.

Late Friday afternoon we were still waiting, and I was growing impatient. For months I had been holding my expressions of love for my baby in my heart, and now all I wanted was to be able to express my love to him in person. Without expecting it, my thoughts shifted to my own mother. How different her frustration must have been.

While my frustration stemmed from lengthy anticipation and delayed joy, hers must have felt more like dread and apprehension. Waiting for a child who was a mistake, an inconvenience, must have weighed on her heart like a stone. And knowing my arrival was probably absent of any joy brought tears to my eyes.

It was such a contrast to the expectancy that had lifted my heart to heights I had never experienced before. As I brushed the tears from my eyes, I was keenly aware that of all the blessings I would ever know, being a mother would be the most significant.

I brushed away another tear, realizing it was a blessing my own mother had never accepted or known.

By evening, the contractions had increased in frequency and intensity, and after a call to the doctor it was decided we should return to the hospital. Although still not dilated enough, I was admitted, and Joe and I spent the next hours walking the corridors of the hospital in hopes of speeding up the process.

Holding onto each other there was a keen awareness we were in the final moments of being just the two of us. In a few hours this duo would be forever changed. We would be more than just husband and wife — we would be father and mother of a newly created family.

As that realization crossed my mind my heart was filled with incredible tenderness toward Joe. This was the man who changed and enriched my life, the man I chose to journey through life with. And soon he would be the man I would raise and nurture a family with. Suddenly my hand in his felt even safer, and his shoulder beneath my head felt even stronger.

As we continued the corridor walk into the wee Saturday morning hours, our excitement was slightly overshadowed by exhaustion, both physically and mentally. As I grew wearier, my mind began to revisit fears that had been woven deep into the fabric of my soul as a child. Even though God had done a miraculous emotional and spiritual healing in my adult life, there were still moments when threads from the past would make their way to the surface.

As a child I had to be a survivor, which meant anticipating and maneuvering through the worst of times. Now in the midst of this joyful and anticipated blessing, I found myself wondering if my future really could be that far removed from my past.

When we returned to the room, I crawled onto the bed and found myself overwhelmed by the conflict inside. I knew without a shadow of doubt that my husband and baby were a blessing from God. He had proven His love and kindness to me time and time again, and at every turn had outdone Himself on my behalf. But the little girl with the haunting memories who still occupied a small corner of my heart knew that something would go wrong.

In her experience, something bad always happened.

I finally mustered the courage to express my fears to Joe. My voice cracked a little, afraid to say it out loud, but more afraid not to discuss the possibilities at all.

What if something happens to the baby? What if he dies? What if I die? What if we both die?

I had worked so hard to make everything perfect. I had followed the doctor's orders, I ate well, I made lists, I followed the lists, I decorated, I hoped, I prayed.

But what if something went wrong?

I felt like the little girl survivor in me had been wound up and let loose, scurrying frantically in search of a safe place. Then Joe smiled, shook his head slightly, and looked confidently into my eyes. His voice was soft and reassuring as he reminded me of the loving God who had redeemed my life for good things. *Good things, Michelle.*

With those words I felt the faith and trust that had taken root in my rescued heart, rising up to quiet the worries in the wounded heart of my past.

Around nine o'clock Saturday morning, several friends I had invited to provide moral support in the family birthing room arrived at the hospital. They were women I had grown attached to since my arrival in Sacramento, and ones I felt would best help me prepare for and navigate the birth experience. Two of them were in different stages of motherhood, so the wisdom of what to expect gave me great comfort.

By that time I had already been in labor thirty-five hours, and with each ensuing examination of my progress, it was apparent that the moment of mommy and son introduction was still some hours away.

As the waiting game continued, the room was filled with respectful enthusiasm and reassuring encouragement. Joe was quietly attentive, keenly aware of my needs moment by moment — rubbing my back, holding my hand, and whispering affirmations that he was proud of me. But the truth was, I was deeply proud of him for how lovingly and patiently he had kept me calm and focused throughout the process.

After the next painful contraction subsided I reached up and touched Joe's face and he gently drew my hand to his lips. As I looked into his eyes I could see an amazing future filled with love and devotion for both myself and our son. With the baby's heartbeat playing rhythmically on the monitor, we smiled at each other, and he kissed my hand again. And as I brought my hand back to my stomach, I stroked it lovingly and marveled at this blessed beginning.

But in that moment of quiet elation I was also keenly aware that not all beginnings are filled with such love and support, and I found myself thinking about my own.

Given the circumstances of my mother's pregnancy, I wondered if anyone was there to stand by her through the delivery. Was the man who fathered me there? Did he even know about me? Based on the information I had gathered over the years the answer to those questions seemed to be no. And from all accounts my arrival became the source of more angst and resentment in my mom's already troubled life.

Over the next hours we were stuck in a cycle of intense contractions followed by moments of complete physical collapse. Though the affirmations were still expressed, I could see a look of helplessness growing on Joe's face. Squatting beside the bed during my moments of rest, he would hold his head in his hands, increasingly concerned about the next painful battle I would face.

There was no question Joe was my hero, my gift. The depth of his significance was powerfully underscored following one incredibly difficult contraction. Once the pain subsided, my body melted into the mattress, and for a brief moment I found rest. Joe was sitting next to the bed with his arms draped over the guardrail and texting my progress to his parents. The room was dimly lit, and when I opened my eyes the only thing I saw was Joe's face illuminated by the light from his phone.

In that moment everything paled in comparison, as if God was highlighting the fact that He had personally chosen, anointed, and appointed Joe to cherish me and lead our family. When he realized I was watching him, he lowered his phone and smiled. It was a smile that summed up all the reasons I loved him, and all the reasons I knew he was God's very best for me.

Time continued to move dreadfully slow. Following another contraction, I laid my head back on the pillow and released a frustrated sigh combined with a slight whimper. As I opened my eyes I looked at the clock again. But this time rather than focus on the slow moving hands, my eyes were drawn to the cross that hung right above it. My heart felt a surge of emotion as I was immediately mindful of God's Son and the pain He had endured. The agony, the anguish, the suffering, the great pain – it was all meant for more.

Even though my body was completely fatigued, my frayed emotions were suddenly revitalized. This pain was meant for more. Soon it would bring forth life. It would all be for Cohen. And I knew as he grew in years and wisdom, Joe and I would be diligent to teach him about the amazing gift of spiritual life God and His Son made possible for all of us.

Just after mid-day I had a contraction that totally

consumed my body, sending me into a rapid succession of pain-filled expressions. With cries of agony, I grabbed the handrail tight and then released it abruptly to bring my hands to my face.

As I cried out, "I don't know what to do," I reached over and grabbed the pillow and brought it up over my face. I held it tight for a moment then flung it away, bringing one hand to cover my mouth and the other to my stomach.

When the pain finally started to subside, I moved my hand from my face to my stomach. As I breathed deeply, allowing my back and shoulders to relax onto the bed, I was suddenly aware of how I had positioned my hands. One rested on top of my stomach and the other just below, as if I was cradling Cohen through the pain and letting him know Mommy was there.

With that realization I was deeply moved, because I knew in spite of what I had lacked in my young life, the mother's heart inside of me seemed to instinctively know that you protect your child at all costs. Suddenly all the questions that had filled my mind about whether I could be a good parent without having a good parent example were answered. By God's grace, I was going to be the loving, caring mom I had hoped and prayed to be.

By ten o'clock Saturday evening, I had dilated some but nowhere close to where I needed to be for delivery. My friends' laughter and conversation had faded and the room was quiet again. The silence magnified the rhythm of Cohen's heartbeat on the monitor, causing me to reflect on the events of the preceding hours. Interestingly, thoughts of the labor pains and agony reminded me of spiritual struggles.

I thought of how often people experience emotional agony and spiritual pain, without ever crossing the threshold into the newness of life God intends. I thought about the struggles in my past, and how dramatically my life changed when I experienced spiritual birth. And in the quietness of the room, as my heart beat in time with my son's, I was so grateful that God's gift of spiritual life had allowed me to become the woman and mother I had once only imagined.

Finally at 12:44 a.m. on Sunday morning, the nurse looked up from her routine check and announced that I was fully dilated and ready to have a baby. Instantly everyone was on their feet. The room, once dim, was now filled with white light and an expectancy that was exhilarating. The nurse left to alert the doctor and returned within moments to prepare the newborn station in the corner, checking the monitoring equipment and warming light. Joe held my hand excitedly and kissed my forehead.

This was the moment we had been waiting and praying for. We were going to be a family in just a matter of minutes.

At that point everything switched into high gear. The nurse spent the next few minutes explaining the pushing process. Joe called his parents in Illinois and established a video feed through his laptop, and my friends were quickly designated to help hold my legs up while I pushed. Then at 12:53 a.m., in the midst of the excitement and exhilaration, we all quieted ourselves, bowed our heads, and together prayed for the birth of the one we had long anticipated.

With everyone in place the nurse asked for six good pushes to gauge how long the process might take. With each push I grabbed my knees, pulled myself forward, and followed Joe's count. After the first push, wanting to make sure I hadn't done it wrong, I asked the nurse if I was a good pusher.

She sweetly confirmed I was doing a good job, and I instantly felt a sense of relief and accomplishment.

In between pushes we waved to Joe's parents. They had been praying for hours and were so excited. And we felt so blessed to have them there electronically to cheer us on and support us, and to welcome their grandson.

Between pushes we also talked to Cohen, and Joe's eyes filled with tears as he spoke his first daddy instructions, "Come on out, little buddy."

Toward the end of the third push, as Joe was counting down, I looked at the nurse and announced, "That's three. Just so everybody knows!"

The room was filled with laughter at my declaration, but I wanted everyone to know I was determined to be holding my son within the number of pushes she had designated.

Finally, the nurse asked for one more small push. Cohen's head was beginning to crown, but the nurse wanted plenty of time to page the doctor for the delivery. After a small push the nurse announced we were close and then quickly disappeared to alert the doctor.

The anticipation in the room was unlike anything I had

ever experienced, as enthusiastic banter paired with the undeniable wonder of the moment. With smiles and laughter and tears we all recognized we had a front row seat to an amazing event. We were all poised to welcome life. And, despite having experienced two days of contractions, my body surged with an energy that would soon make that a reality.

The doctor arrived and positioned himself, and within a matter of minutes and a few more pushes, Joe and I watched him guide Cohen into the world. It was May 5, 2013, at 1:39 a.m.

Everyone in the room cheered. Joe's parents celebrated with tears and hugs. Joe and I were ecstatic. As he leaned over and kissed me, and told me how proud he was of me, I was completely overwhelmed by the favor and blessing my Heavenly Father had shown me in this miracle moment.

But suddenly I realized the excitement amongst my friends had stopped. As I saw the look of concern on their faces, I quickly looked at the doctor. He was holding Cohen and working quickly to separate him from the umbilical cord. But Cohen hadn't cried yet and he wasn't moving. The prolonged labor had resulted in fetal stress and the blockage of his airways.

The nurse rushed from the room and within seconds was back to carry Cohen from the doctor to the newborn station. Immediately she was joined by four or five medical staff, all intently focused on our son. Joe grabbed my hand and the moment stood still. Soon we heard one nurse say to another, "He's not breathing."

The rush of activity continued.

Then another responded, "I'm not getting a heartbeat."

Joe held my hand tighter. I couldn't breathe, and suddenly it felt like my own heart had stopped beating.

The urgency continued in the corner. My view was partially blocked, but Joe watched as the nurses quickly ran suction tubes into Cohen's mouth. I looked at Joe and could see he was frozen with helplessness and disbelief. Then we heard a nurse ask how long Cohen had been in distress. The other nurse turned and looked at the clock on the wall — the clock beneath the cross.

His response was sober, "Eleven minutes."

Hearing no cries, and no sounds of life, fear gripped my heart and mind. It was everything I had dreaded. In my life the important things had always been taken from me. As a child I had been robbed of my identity and purity, in my teen years of my sobriety, and now as an adult, my son.

I closed my eyes and in the most desperate moment of my life pleaded —

"God! "Please do something!"

To this day it is difficult to recount that moment, and to revisit the flood of emotions that were crammed into those ticking seconds. But to fully comprehend the depths of my pleading and the fear of losing all I held dear, it's imperative that you know my story as a whole.

And so we begin.

PART II

The Formative Years

"For in every adult there dwells the child that was,
and in every child there is the adult that will be."

~ John Connolly

2

Without a Father: Abandoned

I was born on January 23, 1980, in Anchorage, Alaska.

I have no information other than that about my birth.

I don't know if I was an easy delivery or if my mother labored for hours.

I don't know if there were visitors who stopped by after my arrival, or if the whole incident was something that caused friends and family to merely shake their heads in disgust and frustration.

I don't know if my name had been carefully considered and chosen, or if it was just a random, last minute selection because the nurse needed to complete the paperwork. I don't know if my mother visited the nursery to check on her new baby girl, or if she simply stayed in her room feeling indifferent toward her responsibility and contemplating *what now.*

My guess would be the latter.

I've often heard mothers sharing the "blessed event" details with their children —how they were first placed on mommy's tummy, and how daddy stood nearby beaming with pride. Given the fact my father could have been one of four men; I think it would be safe to assume the proud and doting father was not a part of my beginnings.

Perhaps the uncertainty of paternity kept any of them from showing up at the hospital. Perhaps some of them never even knew of the possibility. Maybe they did know and simply didn't want to be tangled in the life of confusion and turmoil that had ensnared my mother.

Then again, maybe someone was there. And when all was said and done, he deliberately chose to turn and never look back.

Whatever the circumstance, no father was listed on my birth certificate, and when it came time for my mother to put a last name on the document, her ex-husband's name seemed an adequate solution to the dilemma. My mother had two children with her ex-husband, a boy and a girl. Their last name, the name that I would borrow for lack of my own, was Sterling. Several years after my birth, my mother had her fourth child, and her last name was Kelly.

Although the direction of our lives paralleled as we shared the same mother and experienced the same dysfunction and chaos, my brother and sisters had one distinct advantage over me.

They knew who they were.

For better or worse, their value was established by a father's presence. They could speak the name "daddy" and it had significance. It was connected to someone who had acknowledged them by choice. But I remained the little girl who no one chose. In the ever-changing situations and environments I found myself in, I was limited to temporarily borrowing someone else's dad.

But borrowing rarely satisfies the heart's desire to have a father of your own.

The one time in my young life I came close to having a normal paternal influence was with my mom's boyfriend, Lenny.

She called him Gator.

Lenny was good to my mom and wanted to marry her and take care of us kids. I was only three or four-years-old at the time, but I remember clearly that Lenny was different than other men that had entered our lives. He was nice to us, even dressing up as Santa Claus for Christmas.

But having a father figure, someone to fill the void in my heart, was not meant to be. A Mother's Day gathering found Lenny in the middle of a confrontation with a family friend. After the friend left the house, Lenny went outside to retrieve a pipe from his car. He was planning to lower the bar in our closet so we could reach our clothes easier. As he removed the pipe, the man he had argued with earlier stepped into the driveway, pulled a gun, and shot Lenny.

At the sight of his lifeless body lying on the ground, my little girl hope for a daddy disappeared.

Once again, I was the abandoned one.

My brother and sisters still had their dads, but I lost my chance. It wasn't for me to know the feeling of safety in a father's embrace. I would never experience the elation of showing my accomplishments at an open house. I would never receive a birthday card or Christmas present with "Dad" purposely penned.

As a child, I never dwelt on the losses I experienced, but the truth of that abandonment coupled with my mother's continued indifference and neglect would build a foundation with no other promise but to crumble.

3

Without an Identity: Lost

They're common circumstances —stories of nameless, discarded children who have silently endured a life defined by destitution. They hide in the shadows growing more and more despondent until something forces them from the corners.

When their compounded sense of hopelessness detonates and tragedy strikes, the running commentary explains, "They were lost." Whether lost in "the system" or lost in adversity, the implication is that they have vanished from sight — they are invisible. Their identity is stripped away. Their worth becomes void.

Soon after the birth of her fourth child, my mother began to feel the pressure of parenthood. Her existence revolved primarily around drugs, alcohol, and random men.

The needs of four children greatly complicated the downward spiral she had adopted as her lifestyle. As she abandoned all common sense the neglect increased, and the hearts of impressionable children became lost in the instability. The identities of an entire family quickly vanished into the shadows of pain and confusion.

Most children have the privilege of maturing in stages appropriate for their age, but the environment my brother and sisters and I experienced required a maturity beyond our years. It instilled an awareness of depravity that left no room for innocence or childhood simplicity.

While most children delight at the colors of Christmas lights, I remember our colorful porch lights. The color was changed frequently. Blue was the signal that there were drugs for sale inside the house, and red was the signal nothing was available.

While most children play fort with blankets and pillows in the middle of the living room, I remember scrambling to find safety under musty box springs. On many occasions I lay there barely breathing as the pounding on the front door in the early morning hours signaled the arrival of the police, or a drug dealer intent on settling a score. As the voices in the living room intensified in volume and anger, and as doors slammed and scuffles ensued, there was an innate understanding that I could not move a muscle.

I could not whimper. I could not cry. I could not let the danger in the next room find me.

Generally children have friends or relatives who are concerned about their well-being, but there was no one in my early life who was alarmed by the conditions. No grandparents to raise an eyebrow at my pale face, constantly dirty with dark circles framing my eyes. No uncles or aunts to wonder why my clothes were always soiled and reeking of cigarette smoke.

Living in trailers and run-down houses hidden by trees on the outskirts of town, there were no neighbors close enough to question a young girl's face void of expression.

The people who weaved in and out of my life never looked beyond the moment of the next drug induced high or next drunken stupor. Concern for the young impressionable minds living in the center of the depravity was non-existent. Our fear went unrecognized, our confusion was never addressed, and our innocence and our worth were not protected. In our own home we were invisible, and quite literally, lost.

By the time I was five-years-old, my mother's chaotic lifestyle had taken a toll on her. Anxious to escape the life she had created and could no longer manage, she decided to move to Texas. But first, some house cleaning would be required. And it wasn't a matter of giving away tables and chairs she didn't want to transport. It wasn't about downsizing the possessions accumulated over the years — my mother needed to free herself of her kids in order to start a new life.

I remember the day my mom told us about the "giveaway." She called us into the living room where she knelt almost emotionless next to the tattered sofa. The room was cluttered and dingy. An uneasy quietness seemed to settle over it. It's funny how even young kids can sense when something bad is about to happen.

Even though we were wise beyond our years — even though we had experienced all the bad one could imagine — there was something different about this. Something scary.

There was a random man sitting on the loveseat just to the right of my mom. I knelt between them. I don't remember who he was, but he seemed to know the secret that was about to change our lives. Then, about as matter-of-factly as saying it was Tuesday, my mom told my older brother and sister they were going to live with their dad. Then she told my younger sister she was going to live with her dad. I remember there were tears. Despite the hell we had been raised in, this was our home. It's what we knew.

Then, even as young as I was, the thought crossed my mind, *what about me?*

I didn't have a dad. Where would I go? Who would take me?

Suddenly, my brother and sisters' tear-stained faces were blurred by my own tears. Bewilderment must have crossed my face because my mom suddenly reached toward me, and as if it were a game, she pushed me toward the man and laughingly said, "Here, you take her."

He joined in the game, quickly pushing me back and saying, "I don't want her —you take her."

I remember being volleyed back and forth several times, trying to make myself smile for the game. But with each push, as the words were repeated over and over again, I realized I was alone. I had no understanding that I was growing up neglected and destitute, but I did comprehend I was the kid nobody wanted.

Not long after the giveaway, my mom and I moved Texas. In an odd twist my younger sister and her father came with us. Life continued in the same chaotic rhythm we had always known, with the lives of my siblings quickly fading into insignificance.

Despite her life being less complicated with just two children, my mom's pattern of neglect remained consistent, and we soon became as invisible as my older brother and sister.

Soon after we arrived in Texas, financial problems plagued my mom's relationship with my sister's father. With the living arrangement becoming more and more strained, the decision was made to go their separate ways. Like all his other belongings, my sister was simply packed up and handed to him as he walked out the door. I was devastated. The one remaining person with whom I felt an alliance was torn from my life.

Now, it was just me.

It wasn't too long before my sister's father realized that being a single parent was a demanding job and reluctantly returned her to my mom. But the lure of a new life was quickly highlighting my mom's need for freedom from responsibility. Since caring for young children interfered with the lifestyle she was continually drawn to, there was only one thing she could do: she'd have to give us to someone.

Having done it only months earlier in Alaska, the act

itself would not be difficult. Rather, it was the lack of friends and family that presented the greatest hurdle. But for a person in pursuit of freedom, the problem would be far from insurmountable. One day she simply relinquished her parental rights and gave my sister to people from Ohio.

As quickly as she had been returned to us she was gone. It felt like an aftershock that follows a terrible earthquake. Nothing felt sure or safe...again.

The question surfaced in my young mind once more, "*What about me?*"

That question was promptly answered the day my mom led me up the walkway of a neatly manicured home, knocked on the door, placed my hand in the hand of a stranger, and simply disappeared from sight at the end of the street.

I have no idea if my mom knew this family from years before, or if she had met them since our arrival in Texas. But I remember peering through the screen while my "new mom" tried her best to ease me into the transition. My heart pounded. Suddenly, without warning or explanation, I, too, belonged to a new family.

Surrounded by unfamiliar sights and sounds, I remember sitting stiffly on the edge of the sofa, my feet barely touching the floor. I politely nodded my head when the lady and her husband asked questions and forced a smile when they told me they were happy to have me live with them.

As I sat quietly and twisted the fringe on the throw pillow, my gaze slowly shifted back and forth to the door.

I remember wishing I could put one foot down, then the other, then ease my way across the room, burst through the screen door, and run until I caught up with my mom. But somehow I knew, even as fast as I could run, I wouldn't find her. She was gone.

The only identity I had ever known had been ripped away. I was not just a little girl lost anymore. I was also alone.

As the weeks passed, I adjusted into my new surroundings, although a structured family life was completely foreign to me. I had no idea there was supposed to be a regular time for meals and bed, a routine for bathing and washing hair, or even the right time to place soiled clothes in the laundry.

I certainly didn't realize family life was meant to include parental guidance. So the couple's attempt to teach me Spanish and various social skills was met with a degree of resistance. My long, uncooperative stares evidence that their interest felt restrictive to my untamed spirit.

Through conversations I overheard while living there, I came to understand the couple was not able to have children of their own. So for all intents and purposes, my mother's problem had become the answer to theirs. While there should have been some security in the notion they wanted me, I remember lying awake at night knowing I could never really be theirs. I had a mom. But at the same time it was scary to realize the trade from one mom to another had been made so easily.

During my stay with the couple there was no

communication from my mom. The lady never talked about her, and I didn't ask questions. To this day I still don't know how long I stayed with them. But I do remember as abruptly as I was dropped into their lives, I was just as quickly removed.

It was a weekday morning when my mom showed up unexpected and unannounced and posed the most unfair question to my already confused and deeply wounded heart. She asked if I wanted to stay with the people or come live with her. I remember watching sadness fall over the people's faces, and their eyes begging me to stay. They obviously knew my best chance for a stable life was with them. But because a child is innately drawn to her parent, I made my decision to go. And as my mom matter-of-factly motioned for me to *come on*, I stepped onto the porch and back into a life lost in chaos and depravity.

Even though my mom had demonstrated time and again her preference to be unencumbered, there remained an odd belief that she could exert her parental authority and reclaim her children at will. With me now back in her custody, she decided to exercise that right and reclaim my sister from Ohio. But when her desire was met with reluctance, my mom would make yet another unthinkable decision. She reported to the police that my sister had been kidnapped.

I don't know what transpired from there, but my traumatized sister was eventually returned to Texas, where her paternal grandparents were given custody. I didn't see my sister again for several years, and those circumstances were just as horrific as anything we had experienced before.

4

Without Security: Unsafe

Of all the desires of the human heart, whether young or old,
security is one of the most sought after. Security speaks to safety
and protection and provides opportunity for growth and
development. Without security people become the prey of difficulty
and risk. They constantly struggle to survive.

When the necessity to survive becomes the foundation on
which a young life is built, the struggle often gives way to
unimagined despair and hopelessness.

When I left the couple's home I was about six or seven-years-old. My mom's life had not improved during the time we were apart. In fact, her downward spiral seemed to take an even more twisted and destructive path.

At the time, we were living in a very small apartment,

and my mom had landed a job as a bartender in a local dive. Once again, without family or friends to share in the responsibility of raising a child, my mom made decisions that would require me to develop and engage survival skills never meant for a young heart and mind.

Since I had not yet been enrolled in school, our routine was to sleep during the day. In the late afternoon we would go to the bar, where I was allowed to play on the stools and chairs until the crowd started arriving. Then I would be positioned under the bar and told to be quiet, with an occasional green olive or maraschino cherry handed to me by one of the bartenders.

As I listened to the blaring music and the constant clinking of glasses, I would watch my mom's legs pass by me again and again. Quite often I would watch as she lingered in one spot for longer than normal. Then she would stand more on her tiptoes to better lean over the bar. And while the constant chatter and exaggerated laughter of the crowd made her conversation indiscernible, I became aware that the tiptoes meant my mom would have company that night.

At the end of the evening, more often than not, a man reeking of alcohol would follow us to our apartment, and in the instant the key turned in the lock and the door was flung open, their uncontrolled passion would find them sprawled on the couch, just feet from where I would sleep.

I was never shielded from the display. I was never told to turn away. I was simply left with images that made me feel confused and survival skills that made me feel numb.

As time progressed, I became more aware of feeling

unsafe. I probably didn't know what to call it then, or how to articulate the feelings, but I knew every day I felt alone and unprotected. For many kids feeling unsafe is temporary, the triggering event or situation effectively soothed by the presence and attention of a parental figure.

In my case there was no one I could look to or depend on but myself, so the only option I had was to continue to develop survival skills.

The most significant challenge to my survival came days after a Thanksgiving holiday. My mom had a gentleman friend who was around more consistently than others, and he was at the apartment when I went to sleep that evening.

When I woke up the next morning, the apartment was quiet — but a different kind of quiet. As I looked around I realized no one was there. I opened the door slightly for a peek outside, but saw no sign of my mom or her friend.

With my heart pounding, I nervously sat on the sofa and waited for my mom to come home. I was sure it would be soon. But as I waited, and waited, and as the morning became afternoon, I somehow understood she wouldn't be home.

By the end of the day I realized I was hungry and would have to fix myself dinner. So I sat down at the small, cluttered kitchen table and proceeded to pull dry meat off of the turkey carcass. And as darkness fell, and I ate in silence, I had no idea what I was supposed to do next.

Whatever it was, I knew I would be doing it alone.

The next morning when I woke up I was still by myself. But I wasn't as scared as the day before. Maybe because I knew if I was hungry I could find food. Or maybe because the day felt so much safer than the dark, lonely night I had just survived.

As I sat again at the kitchen table pulling the dry, crusty meat off of the turkey carcass, I knew that if I was okay inside the apartment, I would probably be okay outside, too.

It was during this time I befriended an elderly woman in the apartment complex. She invited me in and served shortbread cookies that were perfectly displayed in little paper cups in a blue metal tin. I don't remember what we talked about. I don't even remember if she asked me questions about who I was or where I lived. But over time her apartment became a safe place I could go when I was left alone or the door to our apartment was locked and I couldn't get in.

Looking back I wonder what she thought as she sat across from the little dirty-faced, tangled-hair girl.

Did she wonder why I was alone so often? Was she troubled there was no youthful spark in my eyes? Was she concerned that no one ever came looking for me? Did she purposely keep cookies on hand for the times the lonely neighborhood waif showed up at her door? Were her acts of kindness offerings of assurance that somebody cared?

I'll never know the answers to these questions, but I do know in those moments spent over cookies, she was my best friend.

My mom disappeared on multiple occasions. Since she returned each time before, I assured myself that if I waited, she would eventually come home. There were times, though, that I thought if I could figure out where she went I could go there, too.

I wandered through the apartment, as if some clue had been left behind. I remember one day wandering into the bathroom and finding a medicine bottle on the counter. The bottle had a picture of an Indian on it, like in the cowboy movies I watched. The liquid inside was red. I thought it was blood, and I remember feeling really scared because I thought my mom had run away to be an Indian. And I knew I would never find her, because I didn't have any idea where Indians lived.

When she came home the next day I cried, relieved I wouldn't be left alone forever.

While we were still living in the apartment, and my mom was still tending bar, she met a man she decided to marry. I don't remember his name, but I do remember they were married in the bar, and the new man soon became my babysitter at night while my mom was at work.

After much practice, I had adapted to the comings and goings of my mom's friends, so accepting a new man in the house was not difficult. The man was nice enough, but it was apparent from his lack of interaction that he had no intention of being my father.

Most of the new man's nights were spent watching TV and drinking beer. And while there was a sense of comfort having someone in the house with me at night, I still felt invisible and alone. I was never afraid of the man, until one night in his intoxicated state he decided to chase me around the room pretending to be a monster.

Happy for the attention I giggled and ran back and forth from the kitchen to the living room. Then it happened. At the height of the fun, the man slipped on a throw rug in the kitchen and landed flat on his back. Immediately, he became infuriated and began cursing and yelling.

I froze.

Then as he continued his tirade and started to get back on his feet, I did what any survivor would do. I hid.

As I huddled nervously in the corner, the man's presence, once somewhat comforting, had now become frightening. I sat quietly, not moving a muscle, hoping his temper would subside and the next beer would make him fall asleep like the times before. When he finally did fall asleep, I tiptoed to my bed, quietly crawled in and covered my head with a blanket. Like every other night that had led up to that one, I fell asleep feeling unsafe and alone.

I don't know how long the man stayed with us after that. But soon after the marriage ended my mom found herself in trouble with the law. I was seven-years-old and had never attended school, so the local authorities were determined my mom would enroll me in kindergarten.

Not far behind that confrontation would be her arrest for writing bad checks and petty theft.

Suddenly I found myself immersed in a classroom environment that was far beyond my comprehension, and adjusting to my mother's abrupt absence.

To this day it is a complete mystery to me where I stayed or who I was with during my mom's early incarceration.

Perhaps it was a time too emotional to remember, or maybe it was a time just easier to forget.

But the loss of security and my fight to survive would take on a whole new meaning with the next careless decision my mom would make.

5

Without a Name: Insignificant

What's in a name? A name is identifying. It gives individuality.
Distinction. A name establishes significance. But when identity is
uncertain, and a person walks through life confused by her worth,
insignificance becomes the resulting theme.

By the time I was eight-years-old, I had routinely used
two last names that never belonged to me. The first was the
last name of my older brother and sister's father. The second
was the last name of my younger sister's father. I even used
the last name of the couple I had stayed with temporarily.

But they were all borrowed names.

Simple to tack on at the end of Michelle, and easily
discarded once my environment changed. The most difficult

challenge presented by the exchanges was simply remembering which one to use.

Because of the continuing neglect and occurrences of "giveaway," the name of "daughter" seemed to hold little importance. To the people who had weaved in and out of my early life I was simply "the kid." To outsiders looking in I was probably known as "she" or "her." *She* looks lost; *her* clothes are dirty; *she* shouldn't be out this late; I wonder where *she* belongs.

And to some I was probably just "the little girl" who should be in school.

None of the names assigned would speak worth into my life, and my young, impressionable heart would continue to deteriorate into insignificance.

When my mom went to jail, she met a woman named Sue. I don't know Sue's crime, but I do know she shared custody of her two children with her parents. While they were in jail together my mom introduced Sue to her ex-husband, my younger sister's father. They made an arrangement. Upon her release, Sue would marry him and assume custody of both my younger sister and me. But the arrangement would do only one thing: further diminish my name and significance. For the next chapter of my life I would be known as a "burden," a "nuisance," and unwanted "baggage."

It wasn't long before it was apparent kids were a strain on Sue's relationship with my mom's ex-husband. Sue had a difficult time coping with the daily responsibility while he was on the road much of the time. As resentment continued to build, Sue soon directed her anger toward the "nuisances" who complicated her life.

It was then that a new level of abuse would be introduced to our lives.

Verbally there wasn't a day that went by we weren't reminded of our status in the home. Sue often told us we weren't hers to love. She was also known to fly into uncontrollable rages, her fury imposed on the "brats" without warning and absent of any mercy.

My sister and I learned quickly to speak in whispers, play quietly, and never ask for things unnecessarily. We didn't understand the concept of walking on eggshells, but became masters nevertheless. There were times when our presence alone would anger Sue, and in those moments we understood that hasty retreat to our bedroom might be our only hope. But as we crouched together in the corner, the sound of furious footsteps nearing our bedroom door would cause our hearts to race. And the door would fly open, the bunk bed frame and mattresses would be turned over, and our very meager belongings would be violently strewn across the room.

The expressions of rage were not limited to belongings and beds. We, too, served as targets for anger and brutality.

Sue would humiliate us by grabbing our hair in one hand and scissors in the other, and then callously cutting chunks out randomly and unevenly. We were often grabbed by our hair and jerked so hard our feet literally left the ground. Then she would viciously yank us back and forth until she decided to release her grip and catapult us into walls and bedposts.

The pain was excruciating. The more it happened, the less we cried.

My sister and I became skilled at dodging flying fists and open-hand slaps. But on occasion our size would be our handicap, her long reach and strong hand would win, and our skinny, pale arms would become the canvas for her rage, the bruises evidence of blind fury. Black and blue marks would often speckle our knees after long sessions of kneeling on raw pinto beans that had been poured on the floor for our discipline.

On one occasion my sister and I were playing quietly in our bedroom, mindful not to irritate Sue and provoke her temper. Our giggles were subdued at first, but as our silliness increased, a rare sense of uninhibited playfulness came over us.

My sister did a silly little dance then quickly scaled the bedpost to the top bunk. Standing on the mattress she bounced a bit, and we giggled. That inspired a bigger bounce, and then another. Lost in the moment we giggled louder, forgetting all about restrictions and consequences. On the next bounce she lifted her hands to touch the ceiling, and then it happened. She bumped the heavy glass light cover from the ceiling. It fell to the mattress then tumbled to the floor with a thud.

Surprisingly, it didn't break.

Immediately we heard furious footsteps approaching the door. My sister climbed down from the bed and stood at attention by my side. Our hearts were racing as the door flew open with great force. It was apparent Sue was angered by the laughter and noise, but we watched her eyes ignite with fury as she looked at the light cover on the floor. When she looked back at us we dropped our heads and stared at the floor. With a vicious growl she asked *who did this?*

I swallowed hard. Without lifting her head, my sister slowly raised her hand.

I looked nervously at my sister, knowing her fate was sealed. But I thought maybe it wouldn't be so bad since the glass just dropped and didn't break. Maybe Sue would just lock us in our room. Without a word she reached down and grabbed the light cover.

My sister and I looked at each other puzzled, wondering what she was going to do with it. Sue grabbed my sister's arm and proceeded to beat her with it until it broke. After she delivered the last brutal blow, she dropped what was left of the weapon and left the room, slamming the door behind her. And my sister and I simply stood in silence, too traumatized to cry. We faced fear daily, but that attack so terrified us we stood frozen, our ravaged spirits disconnecting from the reality of the moment — both unaware that one of us had wet herself.

One form of punishment used with frequency was isolation. We would be locked in our room for hours on end, missing whichever meals occurred during our confinement. On one occasion my sister had been locked in the room for more than a day. I hadn't seen or talked to her since the afternoon before and we were now nearing dinner time of the second day. Several times I had tried to find the courage to whisper through the gap at the bottom of the bedroom door, but was afraid of what would happen, to both of us, if I got caught.

The house felt eerily quiet. The only noises were the sounds that drifted in from outside, and Sue's periodic turning of newspaper pages in the living room. I felt alone and vulnerable, unsure of everything. I didn't know if I'd see my sister again, or when Sue's next eruption would occur. So I did the only thing an eight-year-old would know to do.

I carefully obeyed the silence.

The second day of my sister's isolation was my birthday, although it was really no different than any other day. I had spent most of the day outside wandering in the yard. I leaned against the tree and slowly pulled bark off the trunk, and sat on the grass, breaking it off blade by blade.

Occasionally, I would look up to steal a glance at my sister's window, not lingering too long because of the trouble it could bring. And each time I looked, there was nothing but stillness. No movement in the window. No shadow behind the old sheet that covered it. I remember my stomach felt hollow. The cotton fabric may just as well have been an iron curtain, with fear residing on one side and despair on the other.

Surprisingly, Sue called me in for dinner that night. I was nervous when I sat down, careful to keep my head hung and my eyes fixed on the plate. Typically the table was no place for kids, and my sister and I would often go for days without anything to eat. We were always hungry, and Sue was always vocally resentful of the small portions she did allow.

During dinner that evening the silence continued, and there seemed to be no reprieve for my sister. As the meal neared an end, Sue walked to the sink to scrape off her plate. With her back turned I quickly wrapped a biscuit and a piece of meat in a napkin and slipped my hand under the table. Sue hesitated briefly and stared out the window. I swallowed hard.

Had she seen me take the biscuit? Did she know I was hiding it?

I sat perfectly still, my heart racing. Finally she turned, squinted her eyes, and stared at me intently, as if trying to figure out the difference in my demeanor. When our eyes locked my face felt hot. I knew I didn't dare make a move to bring her attention to the napkin clutched in my hand. Realizing her suspicions were not going to be confirmed, she barked at me to go outside, then turned and left the kitchen.

I sat still for a while longer and watched the doorway for any sounds that would suggest she was coming back into the kitchen. Then I heard the television click on and the sound of Sue settling in the recliner.

I waited a few minutes more.

Finally, when it felt safe, I twisted in the chair, positioned my feet gently on the floor, and stood up slowly, careful not to make the linoleum creak. Softly I tiptoed to the back of the kitchen. Keeping watch over my shoulder I pushed open the squeaky screen door. As my heart pounded, I slowly returned the screen to the closed position, taking care not to let it shut too hard, all the while terrified that Sue's face, red and distorted with anger, would suddenly appear in the doorway.

Finally, with knees and hands shaking I made my way around the side of the house and gently tapped on my sister's window. There was no answer. I looked down at the napkin, now damp from being clinched so tightly. It was dusk and I knew I would be called in soon, so I tapped again.

No answer.

I remember my legs felt like they couldn't hold me up any longer. I wanted to cry. Then finally my sister's small fingers cautiously pushed the sheet aside and peeked through the crack. I lifted my hand, pulled the napkin back slightly, and motioned for her to open the window. Carefully she reached up, twisted the lock, and raised the window just wide enough for the biscuit sandwich to be passed through. That was the worst and best birthday I ever had.

At some point my mom was released from jail. But rather than come and rescue us from the abusive environment, she would simply come to Sue's and stay for a few days, then disappear for weeks on end. During this time my brother and older sister's father abandoned them, and with no other relatives to take custody, they were sent to Sue's to join my mom.

Upon their arrival my mom made a brief appearance and promptly disappeared again to rejoin a man she met in San Antonio. So Sue's home was now filled with the four "unwanted" kids too insignificant to love.

There was also a man, a relative of Sue's, who parked a shabby trailer on the property. We didn't pay much attention to the man, but he always made it a point to step out of the trailer and sit on the rusty step to watch the "little girls" play. Sometimes we would be running and giggling in the yard, only to stop long enough to catch our breath. And I would look over to see him staring, and offering a smile that made me feel uneasy.

Even as a kid I knew the attention felt strange.

I would protectively take my younger sister by the arm and lead her away from the trailer and closer to the house, keeping a watchful eye on him as our play resumed.

But as the days passed, the man would offer lures that neglected and disadvantaged kids find hard to resist.

He had candy and money.

At first he just sat on the rusty step and waited to catch our eyes. Then he would slowly peel back the wrapper of the candy bar, smile, and take a bite. With our undivided attention he would then stand up, walk into the trailer, and close the door behind him.

The next time he would smile and lift the candy bar up as if to say, *want some?* And each day we would find ourselves drawn just a few steps closer.

Soon the enticement overruled the uneasiness, and my sisters and I found ourselves sitting on dirty cushions eating candy behind a locked trailer door. It became obvious very quickly there was a cost for the candy.

One by one we would each pay the price.

Having routinely experienced physical abuse at adult

hands, and understanding we were too small to fight the evil giants, we sat quietly, dreading the actions that would follow. Then we would watch the helplessness and surrender in each other's eyes, knowing he was too big to stop. As I waited to be motioned over, my feet felt glued to the floor, my legs were frozen, and his stern warning that we'd *better not tell anybody* left my voice paralyzed. I remember feeling numb, the fear disconnecting my mind from the unending moments.

I don't remember how many times we were enticed by and succumbed to the lures, but one day as the events unfolded, my brother's suspicions led him to the trailer, and he relentlessly pounded on the door screaming for his sisters.

The man wouldn't unlock the door. He told us to be quiet and warned us again that if we told Sue, she would think we were liars. Then she would have to send us to jail, because that's where "naughty girls" go. I honestly don't remember what happened after that, but I do know the man's secret was exposed that day.

I knew he wouldn't be able to hurt us again.

Soon after the truth was revealed, my sisters and I were taken to counseling where we would use dolls to describe the violations. Despite the repeated explanations that we weren't to blame, I sadly carried the belief that I was a "bad girl" with me for years. Of all the names that had been used by others to define my insignificance, none could compare to the one I assigned myself.

It meant that maybe they were right about me all along.

Around that time, Sue and my mom's ex-husband filed for divorce, and it was decided my younger sister would go with him. Left without a husband and with three kids that didn't belong to her, Sue's resentment continued to build until one day she contacted my mom to come get us. My mom and her boyfriend had already decided to move to Illinois but had not anticipated starting a new life with three children. When they arrived, the negotiations of our fate began.

There was no family for my mom to send my brother and older sister back to, and because accompanying her to Illinois was not in the immediate plan, they were sent to other temporary homes. Since I had no close relatives it seemed obvious that I would go with her, but in a stunning and callous decision my mom asked Sue to keep me.

Even at my young age I was keenly aware that I was the "disposable" one — the easiest one to leave behind. Despite tears and pleading, my mom packed up the older two and drove away leaving me crying at the edge of the lawn.

As the days passed, the physical abuse diminished but the emotional abuse continued. Sue rarely spoke to me and never called me by name. Her indifference at times felt even more painful than the outbursts. Her deliberate silence compounded the feelings of abandonment and loneliness, and served to authenticate my feelings of insignificance.

Every day I was there I hoped my mom would come for me. One day, I found the courage to ask Sue when she thought my mom would be back. I remember sitting next to her and she took my hand into hers. The attention felt unfamiliar, but pleasant at the same time.

As she held my fingers she asked if I knew how to tell how many people loved me. I shook my head but was anxious to know. Then she pointed to the white crescents at the base of her own fingernails and said, "If you count these, that's how many people love you."

I smiled, happy to know the secret. But then I looked at my fingernails. I had only one white crescent.

My heart dropped. I looked back up at her hoping she would tell me that sometimes that's not what it means at all. But without even looking at me, she matter-of-factly said, "Only one."

Then she placed my hand back on my leg, stood up, and simply walked away. I remember staring at my fingers for a long time. My young mind reasoned that since Sue had kept me, she must be the one who loved me.

But why then did I feel so unwanted?

If Sue really was the only one, that meant I had been discarded and forgotten by my mom. As I pushed the screen door open and sat quietly on the porch step, I was suddenly overwhelmed by loneliness and the thought that I was "no one special."

What's in a name? Sometimes ... everything.

6

Without Stability: Shaken

Earthquakes are terrifying. At their center, they shake the ground violently. Their ripples and rumbles create instability that can be felt from miles away. The shock of the sudden shaking leaves a feeling of unsteadiness and lingering fear and concern. It upsets the natural desire for stability — something humans innately struggle to find. When constancy and safety are shaken, the results of the experience can have damaging, long-lasting effects.

I spent a few more months in Texas with Sue, until she decided she couldn't take care of me anymore. She contacted my mom to arrange for the hand-off. Uprooted again, I was soon put on a plane to Illinois to re-connect with my mom and her new husband. My older brother and sister joined us shortly after.

Soon after their arrival, it was apparent that the instability and brokenness of my sister's past had taken her down a very dark road.

With the family in turmoil, and my mom incapable of providing guidance or discipline, she gave my 12-year-old sister up for adoption. I didn't know if I'd ever see her again.

My life in Illinois wasn't much different than anything else I had known up to that point. There was still no shortage of physical or emotional neglect. Drugs and alcohol were prevalent. It took no time to adjust to the new environment, and I soon found numerous roles that allowed me to fit neatly into the chaos.

My mom and her new husband routinely hosted drug and alcohol parties that lasted all night, and it was not uncommon to have people passed out all through the house when I woke up in the morning.

At the age of 10, I was assigned the nickname of "bar maid" for the parties because of my expert ability at carrying a tray of alcohol through a crowded room, collecting my tips along the way.

When the tray was empty, I knew to go back to the kitchen and fill it. At my young age I had become skilled in assisting the addicts and satisfying their addictions —those were the only times my mom seemed proud of me.

I remember one party in particular when a friend from school had come over with her mom. In between our serving duties we sat and watched the rowdy guests, doing our best to make 10-year-old conversation above the blaring music and loud voices. The guests were especially demanding that night, and I had worked to the point of exhaustion. Just after midnight I made my way to my bedroom and crawled into bed.

Around 2:00 a.m. I was abruptly awakened by someone scooping me off the bed and carrying me through the noisy house to a car waiting in the driveway. Before the party, my friend had asked if I could come over to spend the night.

My mom had agreed.

Still groggy and disoriented, I was laid in the back seat while my friend and her intoxicated mom got into the front and secured their seat belts. With the motion of the car I started to drift back to sleep. Within minutes I was awakened by screeching brakes as my body was tossed from the seat to the floor.

Now fully awake I sat up and leaned forward, my hands gripping the back of the front seat. My friend's mom had dropped her cigarette, and when she reached down to find it, she had almost wrecked, bringing the car to an abrupt stop.

I scrambled into the front seat to find the cigarette in hopes of easing the mom's frustration and avoiding another close call. As I climbed over the front seat to return to the back, my friend and I looked at each other, clearly understanding the danger her mom's drunkenness presented. Her mom shifted the car into drive and we continued on our way.

With less than a mile to go to their house, our luck ran out and her mom swerved off the road, slamming into a telephone pole. Because I was not restrained by a seat belt,

I was propelled from the back seat to the front, hitting my mouth on the dashboard before being thrown through the windshield.

The ejection ended abruptly with my frail body crashing into the splintered telephone pole and then falling limply to the ground.

The next thing I remember were lots of voices and red lights flashing in the darkness. There was a lady kneeling next to me. I think she was a resident in the neighborhood.

She was crying.

As I began to regain my senses, I was suddenly aware there was blood in my hair and eyes and mouth. And as I began to spit and sputter, I realized that my tongue felt a gap in my teeth that wasn't there before. I pushed my tongue through it again and again, almost disbelieving what I felt. Then I reached up and discovered to my horror that my tooth had been knocked out when I hit the dashboard.

Despite all of the chaos, that was the only thing of importance to me at that moment.

Going directly against the lady's instructions I remember twisting over onto my hands and knees and desperately searching the ground for my tooth. As she bent down and picked me up to carry me to the paramedics, I remember pleading in desperation that she let me find my tooth. But she quietly shook her head no. As my body finally relaxed into her arms, she and I spent the next few moments simply crying together.

When I arrived at the hospital I was alone — frightened by all the commotion and unfamiliar sounds. As I lay on the gurney hooked up to needles and monitors, I saw the concern on the doctors' and nurses' faces. One doctor reached down to examine my lip and mouth, and commented quietly to the nurse *her tooth is gone.*

I looked into his face hopeful that maybe he knew how to fix it. But instead he mumbled, *that's too bad.*

I looked at the nurse on the other side of me. Maybe she could talk to him about fixing it. But she didn't.

She just nodded, smiled sympathetically, and patted my arm.

In between the examinations and the nurses working to keep me comfortable, they asked who I was and where I lived. I gave them my new last name, the name I borrowed from my mom's new husband, and my phone number, and asked if they could call my mom.

The nurse smiled and assured me they would do that right away, and my mom should be there soon. Unbeknownst to me the home phone had been disconnected.

Hours passed. I was still alone.

I'm not sure who finally made contact with my mom regarding the accident. I don't know if they told her, but she was so high she didn't understand the severity of the matter. Or maybe she did understand, but knew the effects of the illegal drugs could still be detected and she would risk arrest.

Whatever the reason, she didn't come to the hospital that day.

By late afternoon it was evident to the doctors that no

one was coming for me, so they asked if I had grandparents they could call. I responded that I did, and that my grandpa's name was Johnny. They were the parents of my mom's husband, and they had been especially kind to my brother and me whenever we saw them.

I didn't know their phone number and, because their last name was common in that area, it was necessary for the hospital staff to make call after call to find the right family.

Eventually they found the right family and the nurse came to my room to let me know my grandparents were on their way.

I was relieved.

As I quietly waited for them to arrive, my mind was filled with lots of little girl questions.

I wondered where my friend and her mom were. I hadn't seen them since the accident, and I didn't know if they were okay. I wondered why my mom didn't just let me sleep at home instead of sending me with them. I wondered if when I finally saw my mom she would be mad because I told my phone number and interrupted her party.

But as I lay there unrecognizable from the injuries to my face, it was the questions of my worth that would reveal the deepest wounds.

I remember staring at the plain white ceiling as I began to process the truth of the situation.

The truth was, it was hard for my mom to love me before, and now I was broken. Maybe that's why she didn't come. Maybe she already knew she didn't want me. Maybe it was just like my sister.

Maybe people didn't keep broken kids.

First traumatized by the accident, and now shaken by the uncertainty of my future, a deep sadness settled over me. And as the weight of those questions reinforced the instability of my life, I simply turned my face toward the wall and closed my swollen eyes, my tears falling to the pillow one by one.

Details of the accident soon made the local paper, and after my release from the hospital people would routinely stop by the house to catch a glimpse of the injuries.

I would hear their whispers about the swelling and bruises, and comments about the deep gash in my lip and my missing tooth. I knew the swelling would go down and the bruises would fade. I knew my lip would heal. I heard the doctor tell my grandma all those things.

The one thing he never mentioned was my tooth.

There was no fixing it or making it better. It was just gone.

In time the accident became a distant memory, but I continued to struggle daily with the flaw in my appearance. All of my life, the instability I felt had been a result of other people's behaviors and choices. I was merely a recipient of their flaws.

Now I was flawed myself.

Every time I looked in the mirror, the gaping hole in my mouth would restate that fact again and again. Of all the experiences that had ever shaken my young world, this would prove to be the most damaging, because it made me ugly to me.

The little girl who had survived so much had now become her own worst enemy.

The stability I had once found in the recesses of my heart was now shaken and completely destroyed.

PART III

The Facade

"No man, for any considerable period, can wear one face to himself
and another to the multitude, without finally getting
bewildered as to which may be the true."

~ Nathaniel Hawthorne

7

Without Hope: Desperate

There's a classroom exercise used to teach students to add two or more variables together in order reach a specific, concrete answer. It is called "summing up." If one or more of the variables is not provided, the summation becomes complicated. Problematic.

The end result is frustration and anxiety.

Just as the answer is essential to success, the elements are crucial to the answer. When a person who experiences emotional and psychological insignificance has been assigned a problem, it is difficult for them find resolution. They lack a critical element — hope.

Without hope, the effort to "sum up" life's events generates desperation. The right answers seeming illusive and success feels unattainable.

Over the course of the next few years, my home life didn't change. There was still chaos and neglect, and exposure to addictions and unhealthy choices. My mom was still detached, and we still lived with the uncertainties of tomorrow.

The one thing that did change dramatically was my heart.

I had become angry. Not at others, but at myself. And the anger was never more telling than in my school yearbooks, when I would scratch the picture of my face until it disappeared from the page. I hated the way I looked and treated myself with contempt as a constant reminder.

My pre-teen years proved to be particularly difficult. It's hard to imagine that the loss of a tooth could so significantly damage my image.

But it did.

Add the fact that I was behind in school, almost twelve years old in the fourth grade, and the flaw only complicated matters. I was desperate to fit in but quite obviously out of place.

While most kids that age are looking to be popular and accepted by their peers, my sole desire was to be normal. Ordinary, typical, just like everyone else. But my life's circumstances made that dream impossible. Even at my young age, I sensed I had no control — not over my appearance or my environment or my family. And for the first time in my life I experienced an emotion that rooted me even deeper in hopelessness.

It was shame.

I was embarrassed and humiliated by a life I couldn't change. I was desperate to be anyone but me. It was a weight my young heart was not equipped to carry — a weight from which I had no hope of breaking free.

After some time, it was decided the prominent gap left by the missing tooth should be addressed. I was elated at the possibility of some normalcy. I remember standing in front of the mirror and smiling, slowly turning my head side to side and visualizing a new smile. I imagined classmates greeting me with, "Hi, Michelle," instead of "What happened to you?"

I daydreamed about people saying I was pretty instead of whispering because I wasn't. For the first time in a long time I smiled at the face staring back at me in the mirror. I felt a sense of relief: no more stares, no more questions, and no more curious reactions.

But that anticipation was quickly met with unwelcome results. The temporary tooth stuck out more than any bucktooth could. Upon returning to school, I was met with more whispers and snickers than before. And the cruelty of one particular boy who reveled in constantly calling me "tooth" in front of my peers, was like a sock in the stomach each time he shouted and laughed. The hope I had finally experienced for some normalcy was not just broken — it was crushed. It was as if there was no way to fix the damage that defined me.

Eventually the bucktooth was replaced by a temporary flipper tooth. While it was less noticeable, it still did little to satisfy my heart's longing to feel whole. The flipper tooth was not meant for permanence, it could easily be removed, particularly when it presented eating difficulties. I would simply place my hand over my mouth while I ate to conceal the gap.

I remember one lunch hour at school when the tooth was discreetly removed and laid on a napkin. After the meal was finished, the napkin was accidentally thrown away with the tooth crumpled inside. As soon as the mistake was realized, I panicked. It was as if I was 10-years-old again, transported back to the scene of the car accident, terrified to have my brokenness exposed.

Desperate to find the tooth, I frantically pulled garbage from the big plastic receptacle. It didn't matter that I was elbow-deep in other people's garbage, or that food scraps were smeared on my hands. I had to find the camouflage that had hidden the real me.

At that moment, I was as relentless as a search and rescue dog, and as vulnerable as the one being sought. Finally I found it. I was so relieved.

As I breathed a sigh of elation, my eyes raised to meet the quizzing eyes and obvious whispers of on-looking students. My fear of exposure had left me open for all my peers to see. I was humiliated.

It wasn't long before the new degree of embarrassment demanded stronger armor. It's interesting how the innocence of a child's heart often allows her to go from ouch to ouch without making her emotionally hard. But when innocence is constantly battered and finally destroyed, the child is faced with the realization that pain brings harm. The only way to maintain is to guard their vulnerability fiercely. The armor is cold and hard, providing an opportunity to hide and a place to get lost in despair.

There was no greater indication of the armor I had donned than a photo of me on an Easter Sunday. Standing with the other kids in front of a church, I was almost arms-length away from the girl to my left.

My hip was thrust to the side, my hand planted firmly at my waist. My lips were clinched tight and my eyes intently focused forward. The expression of my toughening heart was unmistakable. The flash of the camera had captured the undeniable truth that my young heart was robbed of hope.

As if losing hope wasn't enough, during this time of self-loathing and desperation to belong, I was dealt an emotional blow that would make me question for the first time who I was. There was no clear answer, because all the necessary components for the equation had changed. The pieces that were meant to fit together to define me — to make sense of my life — were no longer mine to keep.

It was Sue. She and her two children were in a terrible car accident and were killed on impact. I was in disbelief. I argued, insisted that everyone spreading the story was wrong. It was a newspaper article that confirmed the unimaginable tragedy.

There was a part of me that understood that had I stayed with Sue, I would have been in that car, and most probably killed, too. But there was this other part that felt stripped of a major piece of my identity.

The connection to a part of my life, no matter how

dysfunctional it was, was suddenly gone. Any future hope of putting the pieces of my life together to form a whole ended with that news. The snatching away of those months and experiences left me desperate to understand who I would be without that thread in my life's tapestry.

After the news about Sue, I remember walking in a daze for the next few weeks. I felt hollow inside, somehow sensing that happiness wasn't meant for someone like me. With that realization came a decision to protect myself from any further pain.

Pretend you're okay.

Act like nothing hurts.

Conceal the desperation.

Never acknowledge the place where your heart lives is dark and bleak.

Summed up — be someone other than yourself.

In my effort to pretend, I joined the eighth grade cheerleading team. Very quickly I learned it was the perfect platform for appearing cool and together, and it afforded me a much needed sense of status when I was appointed team captain. On the outside I had changed everything, but on the inside, all was still hopeless.

As hard as I tried to convince myself otherwise, I still knew it. The pretense and desperation began to react like oil and vinegar, and I found myself turning an unfamiliar corner. For the first time ever, I was prepared to shrug off and dismiss consequences for my *own* actions.

The first glaring evidence of this change of heart was on the school bus returning from a cheerleading event. Fully understanding the rules of conduct, but not caring about the outcome of crossing that line, I pulled out a package of matches and began to light them on the bus. The gasps of my teammates were impressive, their disbelief somehow fueling the careless attitude my mind had embraced.

It was as if in that moment my role, my façade, went up with the flame. For those few minutes there was a sense of relief, because I didn't have to act. With the first strike and then the next, I was temporarily transparent, uncharacteristically demonstrating my confusion and frustration for having to walk through life without hope and in disguise.

Almost immediately after the incident I was called into the principal's office and stripped of my role as cheerleading captain. I was sorry for losing my esteemed title, but not for the action that led to my dismissal. I nonchalantly reasoned that I could maneuver my way back into a prominent role the following school year after the infraction was forgotten. What should have been a moment of concern regarding my heart's direction simply became an unfeeling, uncaring response.

With hope removed from my life's equation, the unacceptable had become tolerable and the questionable seemed less offensive. The emotional armor that shrouded my heart had allowed me to feel little and express less. With desperation now trivialized, denial had become my norm.

As I continued through my junior high and early high school years, the change in my heart made it easier to fit into the dysfunction of my home environment. Drugs were more prevalent, and parties appealing to all types of addictions were the norm. Because of their need for drugs, and the appeal of profiting from drugs, my mom and her husband soon began dealing as well as using.

With my brother and me in school, we were eventually initiated into the role of supplying eager classmates ready to experiment. There were also times I would sneak the drugs out of the house and simply give them to my friends, all in hopes of feeling cool and accepted. It was quite common for me to board the bus with drugs in my pockets, ready for distribution between classes or at lunch time. Soon, passing drugs became as natural as sharing a stick of gum.

Even though I had witnessed firsthand the effects of drug use, and had experienced some of the most unthinkable circumstances as a result of addictions, my heart and mind had disconnected from the consequences.

Without hope for a life beyond what I knew, I distanced myself from the pain I experienced as a child and resigned to life as it played out. Questions of right and wrong were no longer asked. Consequences were no longer weighed. Life was muddled. It made no sense, and the sum of its parts held no answers. It was quite apparent at my young age that the spiral of despair that had swallowed my mom and her husband had subtly begun to pull me in as well.

The deeper our environment became entangled in the drug culture, the more risk we were exposed to each day. Angry drug dealers would show up on our doorstep in the middle of the night.

Strung-out users, rendered reckless by their high, would

flop at our house. My friends from school would stop in and score, some dancing dangerously close to overdose. When it seemed our environment could get no more out of control, no more irresponsible, we would always move one step closer.

I remember the occasions my brother and I accompanied my mom and her husband to East St. Louis in the middle of the night to pick up drugs. I watched matter-of-factly as the spare tire was removed from the trunk. I listened for the sound of the metal crow bar hitting the dark pavement after the tire was removed from the rim. The whispers and quick moving figures implied urgency. The sound of the packages being shuffled between hands and pressed into the hollow tire was indication the deal was nearly complete. Then the tap of the tire back onto the rim and the closing of the trunk was our cue we would soon be on our way.

Looking back now, I can visualize myself, that hope-starved girl, standing indifferently in the darkness. I see her waiting in the night air, the coldness penetrating not just her bones but also her soul. She is bathed in the numbness that came from years of confusion, feeling little because she had been desensitized to right and wrong. I see her watching with eyes that never knew innocence.

Her view of life defined by the brokenness she witnessed for years. I see her surrounded by shadows and unknown risks lurking in dark alleyways and corners. The answers of her future shrouded because she didn't fully grasp the elements of her present. And then I see her climb back into the car, ready to complete the round trip of despair and emotional desolation.

In the summing up of life, as in the classroom, there are often hints that make the answers more tangible than they might have otherwise been. Advice and guidance shared by someone who understands that the search is difficult often provide the glimmer of hope needed to press on. The advice and guidance may not be used in the moment. And struggle may continue. But the hope of overcoming can never be diminished.

I didn't know it at the time, but in the midst of all the chaos I called life, the people who had become my surrogate grandparents (my mom's husband's parents) had been faithfully praying that God would rescue my family from the vicious cycle of addiction and bitter despair.

I remember one occasion as my mom and I sat in their living room, my grandma began to share about a God who so loved us that He gave His only son to make sure we could live in Heaven one day with Him.

I don't remember understanding it much at that time, but to my young, desperate heart, understanding it was irrelevant. Just the thought of someone loving me that much, and making me clean for the first time, made me want to do what was necessary to meet Him.

So there on the sofa, on October 10, 1992, the three of us bowed our heads as my grandma led us in a prayer of forgiveness and renewal. I'm not sure if my mom went along with the prayer out of obligation or momentary desperation,

My Beautiful Grandparents

but for me it was a heartfelt acceptance of the chance God wanted to give.

It was hope.

It was the piece of the equation that finally made life's answer a possibility.

Although my acceptance of the gift was sincere, my understanding of God's continued presence in my life to guide and restore was limited. For the next several years I remained in the same environment, engaged in the same activities, and walked in the same confusion.

Despite the continued struggle, despite the waywardness that only increased, I somehow sensed that

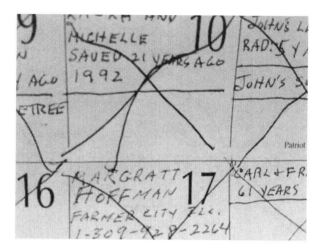

My Grandparent's calendar marking the day I got saved.

moment on my knees would be an important part of the summing up.

8

Without Trust: Alone

People do not thrive when they are isolated and stand alone. But when the reality of life is expressed through careless acts, disregard, and deceit, standing alone often seems inescapable.

There must be trust to stand with others. Trust that they will protect you, and a belief that they will not abandon you when given a chance.

From a very young age I experienced neither trust nor loyalty. Standing alone seemed far less risky than trusting, and far more appealing than being disappointed or exposed.

Over time, my brother and I became more heavily involved in substance distribution to our friends and classmates. We were constantly and forcefully warned by my mom and her husband not to expose the secret to teachers or those in authority. We became experts at trusting no one, and increasingly weary from bearing the secret in painstaking silence.

I remember often sitting in class wondering when I caught the teacher's eye if they knew. I worried if there was something in the way I carried myself or talked to my friends that would give the secret away. For the most part, I didn't trust the teachers' interest in my grades or their inquiries into how I was doing; instead, their concern made me nervous and suspicious.

There was a moment when the burden of silence became far too heavy to bear, and I finally expressed the desperation of my home life to a favorite teacher. I was still afraid of repercussions should my mom and her husband find out I *snitched*, so I spoke in vague terms, careful not to mention the drugs.

I remember her staring at me, lost in how to respond or what to do. I had handed her my trust, and in her bewilderment, she handed it right back as she assured me *things will be okay* and then turned and went to class. Once again, the reality that I was in this mess alone was underscored.

With that momentary cry for help going unanswered, I decided it would never again benefit me to expose my heart. As I began to understand more clearly the ramifications of any transparency or confession, I became more guarded, shutting any doors that may have offered support and made escape possible.

I was desperate. I continued to search for avenues of emotional escape. I was aching to feel different inside. But when that seemed all but impossible, I began looking for ways to simply act differently on the outside. Determined to give the *appearance* of being confident and secure, I decided to join the high school track team and cheerleading squad. Looking back now it's interesting to think I could have chosen a dozen other activities: basketball, softball, tennis, or choir. But I chose a sport that encouraged me to run, and an activity that demanded a happy persona.

For so long, life's circumstances left me standing alone. I was good at it. I learned convince other I was fine, but I didn't like the person I was alone with. Every time I took my mark at a track meet, every time I heard the pop of the starting gun, it was an opportunity to run from me.

With every stride I wanted to be further from the life that was draining my soul and leaving me hollow. I wanted to outrun the hopelessness and desperation that overshadowed me. I wanted to leave the emotional and psychological pain behind me, so far behind that it could never catch up.

With every burst of energy I wanted to believe that I could break free from the chaos and confusion.

With every labored breath and burning muscle I pushed myself harder for the win, in hopes that breaking through the tape with arms raised high would liberate me from my past and my present.

But each time I crossed the finish line, despite the cheers and applause, my heart understood I had run nowhere fast. As I stepped to the sidelines to walk off the track, I felt even more alone. I knew that despite my best efforts, I would always finish as the same me.

Perhaps that's why the idea of the cheerleading was appealing. The squad members were required to be perky and peppy and to always wear a smile. It became a great hiding place for someone who felt so alone. I could put on the uniform, highlight my eyes and cheeks with make-up, and then smile convincingly for the crowds. Fortunately, I had received a monetary settlement from the car accident I was in years earlier and immediately opted for braces to ensure my smile was even more convincing.   Since track hadn't allowed me to effectively run from myself, being a cheerleader was an opportunity to disguise myself.

I gained more popularity and acceptance among my peers and had become a master at playing the role of happy and carefree. But the disguise required on-going maintenance, the tedious job of always making sure the role was believable. The truth was, the life I lived away from school was ugly, and constant effort was required to ensure the worlds of charade and reality never intersected.

I remember an occasion when the coach pulled me aside to ask if I had been smoking. I hadn't. But the thick cigarette smoke that hung in my house and penetrated every thread of my clothing prompted the question. I was mortified.

I couldn't afford to lose my spot on the team, and I didn't want anything to tarnish the positive reputation I had worked so hard to build. But more than that, I couldn't risk someone finding out about the mess I called, "home."

I quickly denied the accusation; concerned the coach

might want to talk to my parents. We stood eye to eye for a moment, the coach searching my face for honesty, my face burning with fear of exposure. Finally the coach gave a nod that she accepted my answer, and my shoulders dropped with relief. But in that moment it was undeniable that the reality of my broken life had intruded into my carefully managed façade.

From that moment on I worked hard to prevent questions and rid myself of all evidence of a troubled existence. I couldn't risk a concerned teacher or coach examining my life because I couldn't trust anyone with its secrets.

In the evenings before bed I would wash my clothes in the bathtub, praying the smell would disappear with each scrub. I remember kneeling and leaning over the tub's edge night after night, tears of frustration dropping into the soapy water as I listened to the family chaos through the closed door.

In those moments I was truly alone because I was the only one in the house who longed for something different, something better, something clean and new.

One night as I wrung out the clothes and gathered them to my face, I realized the stench of the smoke had never been nor could ever be completely washed away in that environment.

Defeated, I sat down on the bathroom floor and slumped against the cabinet. With my head in my hands, I contemplated what to do next. But there was nothing to do. The thing that should have worked, the repeated scrubbing and rinsing, hadn't. With that I sat up straight and banged the back of my head against the cabinet several times in frustration. Then I reached up and pulled a clump of my long blonde hair to my nose. It was in my hair, too. I choked back a groan.

Everything about me was tainted.

In spite of all my efforts to appear different, to *be* different, I had not escaped life's mark on me. I was angry at the unfairness of it all and tired of going through the motions that everything was okay. So that night, as I unlocked the bathroom door and returned to my room with an armful of damp clothes, I made a firm decision that I would take control of my life no matter the cost.

Concerned about improvement in my appearance, I befriended a girl across the street who arranged for me to take showers at her house. When her mom's curiosity was peaked at the number of times I showed up during the week, I'd simply explain that our shower was broken or that our water pressure was low.

Probably seeing right through the charade and recognizing the need, my friend's mom welcomed me in and often offered to launder my clothes. And on several occasions when she bought her daughter clothes, she would buy extra so that I would have a new outfit as well.

The exposure to a normal family life, where care and consideration was openly expressed, made me want to distance myself further from my own home. Compared to other houses on the street, it was apparent ours was neglected on the outside and disorderly on the inside, and going forward I didn't want that environment to be associated with me.

I began getting up early every morning and walking to another school bus stop on another street so the kids would never figure out where I lived. Rain or shine, I would make the journey just to control their perception of me, and to reinforce my façade.

Keeping up appearances had its perks. I liked the fact that people thought I had it all together. I was accomplished in sports and enjoyed a newfound popularity with my peers. I had finally succeeded in changing my image and was no longer thought of as the girl from *that* family or *that* environment. On the outside I had been diligent to always present myself as a confident, successful, happy teenager.

Though the changes I made to improve my appearance and save face were significant in preventing questions, they did little to relieve the frustration that continued to grow in my heart. I had taken control of external things, of situations, but still had no control over the aloneness I felt.

I began to despise the façades I needed to hide behind, but desperately feared letting them go. I was reaching a point in my life where little mattered because little had changed on the inside.

The truth was I felt I couldn't trust myself anymore. The person I had been, the only person I had depended on for years, was disappearing before my eyes. I was lost in my role and I didn't know my lines anymore. All I was really sure of was where I came from and what I'd come through, the brokenness of my family was the only truth I could trust.

Oddly enough, it felt like the very people I was trying to move away from were the only people who gave my identity some stability.

Even that warped sense of belonging was eventually destroyed. With the increasing dysfunction and continued drug use, my brother had developed extremely violent tendencies. His moods would swing dramatically with little or no warning, and once the fuse was lit, the physical outbursts and verbal intimidation and threats were never far behind.

In a moment of rage it was not uncommon for him to recommend I sleep with my eyes open, or to imply an unfortunate accident may happen during night.

In the house where we were living at the time, my bedroom had two doors. One opened out to the living area of the house, and the other into a bathroom between my bedroom and another room. On many nights I would tie a rope to the knob of the bathroom door and secure it tightly to the doorknob on the other side of my bedroom so that he couldn't enter in the darkness.

It was terrifying to realize that the only safety from this danger, was the safety I created. Every late night creak in the floor was a reminder that I could trust no one. The pounding of my heart after the sound of the jiggled doorknob reinforced the truth that I was alone. It was apparent I didn't belong in my own home.

Many years after being given up for adoption, my older sister came to visit us in Illinois. Unfortunately, the years had not been kind to her and had not brought resolution to her tumultuous past. When she arrived she was even more defiant and reckless than when I had seen her last.

Quickly, she re-entered the ugliness of the family dynamic and almost immediately instigated more confusion and chaos. With my brother heavy into drug use, and my sister eager to participate, the despair and depravity of family life was primed to hit new lows.

As I watched an environment that had known no boundaries spiral even more rapidly out of control, I had the sense to know that this new direction had encroached upon and crossed lines that would allow no return. After my sister's visit ended, and she had returned home, I approached my mom to share my uneasiness.

Without a second between my heart's expression and my mother's furious response, I knew that trusting my conscience had sealed my fate. Hearing my mom's angry rant in response to my concerns, my brother quickly descended upon the living room with blind fury.

Like a gazelle alerted to a predator, I knew my survival now rested entirely in my own hands.

Sprinting from the house into the front yard, I could hear my mother screaming and my brother yelling obscenities. I was just past the steps when I heard rapid footsteps behind me. It was my brother. His face was distorted with rage. The vulgar names he was calling me were coming from deep within, like the growl of a rabid animal.

I ran faster, dodging to avoid his grip, pleading for mercy and apologizing as tears of terror streamed down my face.

Understanding his relentless determination to catch me, I quickly reasoned that I should run to the safety of a neighbor, or maybe to the car in the driveway. I thought that if I could at least make it to the car, I could lock myself in until the anger died down. But I was also frighteningly aware that once there, I had only seconds to open the door, close it behind me, and reach around to secure the rest of the manual locks.

I slammed against the side of the car with great momentum. Reaching for the door handle, my hands shook uncontrollably as I fumbled to press the button. It felt like a hundred horror movies I'd seen. The girl struggling to open the door of escape as the madman closed in. Finally the door sprung open and I lunged across the seat. But it was too late. The adrenaline of my terror would prove useless against the power of my brother's rage, as he lunged in right behind me.

Suddenly I was on my back and he was straddled across me, his face blood red and his fists flying in all directions. I turned my face and covered my mouth with my hand, praying he wouldn't damage the smile I had waited so long for.

As I reached up with the other hand to block the punches, he grabbed my wrist, violently moving it to clear the target. The vicious pounding continued for what seemed like an eternity.

My muscles burned as my arms and legs weakly kicked and thrashed against his unrelenting strength. My breath was shallow and labored as my ribs were crushed under his weight. As I twisted my head to look back at the porch, desperate for intervention, I saw my mom watching the attack, as if I had it coming to me.

Never in my life was there a time when I was more alone. Not just alone, but knowing in that moment I mattered to absolutely no one.

Thankfully the neighbors had witnessed the incident and called the police. The sound of sirens getting closer was the hope I clung to and the only connection with reality that finally made my brother end his attack and retreat from the car.

Exhausted, his hands and clothes spattered with blood, he tried to stagger into the house to avoid apprehension. But the police quickly restrained and handcuffed him and arrested him for assault. My mom was furious, trying desperately to explain to the officers that it wasn't my brother's fault, but that I had provoked the outburst.

After the police left I sat on the porch for a long time, wishing in some delusional way that someone, anyone, would come out and check on me.

But that didn't happen.

Eventually I mustered the physical strength and emotional courage to go back into the house, with every intention of fleeing again, if necessary.

My body trembling, and my muscles rebelling against each movement, I stood apprehensively at the screen door. Cautiously I pulled it toward me and was immediately overwhelmed with the hostility that shrouded the house.

My mother's cold stares followed me intently across the living room as I hobbled toward my bedroom, grimacing in pain. The angry mutterings, magnified by the silence, unnerved me, making me fearful for my safety through the long night ahead.

Gingerly I lowered my severely bruised body onto my bed, my mind struggling to comprehend the reality of what had just happened and racing to figure out what I should do next.

I laid there all night in complete solitude, the smallest movement sending waves of excruciating pain through my entire body. Unable to sleep, I watched for hours as the shadows on the wall moved from the dark, desperate night to dawn. And as the light of a new day streamed in, I was deeply aware that between my mother's animosity and the anticipated grudge from my brother, it would no longer be safe for me to stay in the house. Struggling to sit upright on the edge of the bed and shove a few belongings into a plastic bag, I realized that I was now, for the first time in my life, homeless.

9

Without Direction: Adrift

Aimless. Pointless. Wandering. Much like a discarded plastic bag swept up by the wind. Tossed and tumbled, it drifts at the whim of the breeze. No destination ahead, and often damaged and torn by the obstacles it has encountered. Far from its intended purpose, the plastic remains empty and lost until one day it can drift no further.

I was only sixteen, and my life had become no different than a discarded plastic bag.

Within a few days of my brother's arrest, he was out on bail and back at the house. By that time I had retrieved most of my belongings and was staying exclusively with different friends from school. Over the years, I had already begun staying intermittently with friends who opened their homes, staying just long enough not to wear out my welcome then move on to the next open door.

Now, with the permanence of the situation, it was unsettling to know I would never have a place to go back to or refer to as home again.

Even though I made a physical break from my family, there was always an expectation that I owed them my loyalty in the middle of their mess. They resented me for my independence, yet quickly learned how to manipulate me and use that strength for their benefit. Because of all I'd learned to portray, they saw me as a "have," while they remained the "have not's." I watched how my value was measured in direct correlation to their crisis.

About a week after my brother was released from jail, he, my mom, and her husband were all arrested on drug charges. A young man in my high school had gone to the house on his lunch break to buy drugs. He left high, and just blocks away from the house he was involved in a serious car accident.

After establishing where the young man got the drugs, the police arrived and swept through my mom's house, confiscating large quantities of drugs and paraphernalia.

As soon as bail was set, I began receiving calls from my mom demanding that I come get them out of jail. Once my grandparents were able to secure the money, we posted bail for my mom and her husband. Because of my brother's previous arrest, he was not eligible for bail.

On the ride home there was little conversation. No talk

of repercussions or consequences. No discussion of making changes or improvements to their lives.

No hint of remorse for the young man who was injured in the crash.

No sense of responsibility for all the other high school kids, including my boyfriend, they'd supplied to and done drugs with.

Nothing but angry silence.

They were angry with me, at the police, and for the disruption to their lives.

When we arrived home, my mom immediately began searching the house for drugs in the disarray the police left behind. She had gone days without a fix. She searched all the normal hiding places, coming up empty. Desperate, she dropped to her hands and knees. I watched speechless for a moment, wondering if I was witnessing my mom's "rock bottom."

Instead of expressions of helplessness or cries for help, I watched as she began to frantically separate the strands of carpet in hopes that particles of cocaine had been dropped during the police seizure.

Never before had I witnessed such a display of addiction. As her search intensified, she began screaming and cursing as she threw items across the room. There was no rationale, no logic — just relentless determination.

It was as if she had lost a diamond in the sand and was desperate to recover it.

Finally convinced nothing had been dropped or left behind in the living room, she and her husband went into the bedroom and resumed the search through their scattered belongings.

With a sudden shout of elation and excitement, they discovered the police had missed a stash of cocaine in a vase that stood in the corner. With hands raised in celebration and an expression of gratitude for police oversight, they immediately did what they lived for and got high.

Despite my desire to leave, I stayed a few more minutes putting cushions back on the sofa and attempting to straighten the mess that was left behind. As I stood in the middle of the room, observing the collapse of lives, I felt as if I were sucked into a moment of nothingness.

I was standing in an environment absent of any kind of hope, an aimless existence with no sense of purpose or direction. Glancing at all the disorder around me, I wondered how many more chances their choices and lifestyle would afford.

If they died as a result of this current fix, what, if anything, had their lives meant?

I had no answers, just more unsettling questions.

My mom's voice cut through the silence, calling me to come to her bedroom. When I reached the doorway, I expected she might need something, but instead she simply told me to go. I had served my purpose with the bail and the ride home.

My usefulness was replaced by the relief the drugs promised. As I took one last glance at my mom, I realized the environment wouldn't be changing any time soon. She and her husband would just keep drifting from one day to another, from one high to the next, both going nowhere fast.

As I sat in my car and turned the key in the ignition, I replayed the scene inside the house in my mind. Suddenly I had the sense of quicksand. My mom and her husband were being pulled under inch by inch, sinking deeper every day, and they had no idea they should be reaching for a lifeline to keep them from being swallowed alive. Physically, mentally, and emotionally they were losing more of themselves every day.

I shook my head in frustration, wondering how anyone could be that oblivious to what was happening.

As I drove away that day, I was completely unaware of the stark similarities in our lives.

I, too, had been drifting through life.

I had involved myself with endless activities and projects, but it was all for the sake of staying busy and portraying a confident, well-adjusted persona. The fact was, I had no direction.

The confusion, self-loathing, and complexity that defined my life had never been addressed. Emotionally, I just kept drifting, hoping to get further and further from the pain and ugliness. And the care-free persona I had worked so carefully to sculpt and maintain was the quicksand that was swallowing me alive. As I switched on my blinker to make my final turn, it was crystal clear that I was blind to the truth. While I thought I knew where my life was headed, I, too, was going nowhere fast.

Not long after the arrest, my brother, my mom, and her

husband were in court to be sentenced for the charges. My brother and my mom's husband were sentenced to multiple years, while my mom was sentenced to a short amount of time in jail followed by house arrest.

In the meantime, the authorities boarded up the house to deter the dealers and users from returning.

Despite the boarding up, my mom insisted that I find a way into the house so she could make collect calls to me. So one day after school I stopped at the house, discreetly walking around to see how securely the barriers were attached. At the back of the house, I found a door that had not been adequately secured and determined I would use it to inconspicuously make access every day.

I was leading this conflicting double life. At school I was the popular girl without a care; happy, energetic and destined for success. But as the final school bell rang, it signaled the emergence of the girl no one knew. I was the girl who would smile and wave good-bye to her friends, then sneak undetected into the darker, seedy side of life.

I remember the first time I entered the house to wait for my mom's call. My heart pounded as I glanced repeatedly to my right and left over my shoulders to make sure no one spotted me making access.

Once inside, the house was cold and dim, with small streams of sunlight breaking through the gaps in the boards. It was eerily quiet, and it made me feel tense and uneasy, like waiting for the monster to jump out of a dark corner in a horror movie. I sat on the sofa next to the phone and watched the dust particles drift aimlessly in the beams of light.

I listened to the deafening ticking of the clock; anxious for the call to just be over with so I could return to the life I had worked so hard to create.

Every day like clockwork, my mom would call. Every time, immediately after accepting the charges, she would proceed to yell at me for not finding a way to get her out of jail. It didn't matter that it was an irrational request — she just wanted the inconvenience to be over.

I don't remember how many times I went back to the house before she was transitioned to house arrest, or how many times she implied I was worthless for not doing enough to gain her early release. But I do know that's when my mom and I finally went our separate ways.

I was now alone. Totally on my own. I began working multiple jobs to get by. I continued my involvement with track and dance at school, but was formally removed from the cheerleading squad months earlier — most likely because my uniform consistently smelled like cigarette smoke.

Whatever it took — additional jobs, new activities, more diligence — I was determined to prove to everyone around me that I had my life under control. And I was determined to prove to myself that I was the complete opposite of my mom.

All my determination couldn't change the truth that my damaged heart had no direction. On the inside I was aimlessly drifting, being tossed and tumbled by my painful and unresolved past. And all my best efforts to be in control were merely proving an empty point because I had no control.

I was simply going through the motions, while the winds of confusion and frustration continued to carry my emotions far from a place of healing and restoration.

A life adrift can have many different looks and a multitude of end results. But one truth remains consistent for all: a life without direction can never be managed, and a heart without direction can never be at peace.

While on the outside my life looked much different than my mom's, the truth was we had the same drifting hearts that would eventually lead us to the same desperate place.

10

Without Truth: Masked

Years ago a song hit the pop music charts that described the pain behind the mask of a clown. The background music was reminiscent of a circus, with pipe organs and tambourines setting a happy, carefree tone. But the lyrics were quite different. They spoke of a life without truth – the entertainer's smile meant to fool those around him. He sang of the art of disguise and cover-up – his carefree appearance used to camouflage his overwhelming sadness. And the cost incurred for this dishonesty and concealment – heartache and isolation.

When I graduated from high school, I was working three jobs and had severed almost all ties with my mom. Leaving high school was harder than I expected, for the simple reason that it had been my stage for four years. My peers and teachers had been my audience, and for the most part, I had put on one amazing show.

I had successfully concealed the truth of my chaotic past, the angst of my present, and quite skillfully convinced everyone around me that life was good.

Concealment was easy.

The difficult part was making myself believe that neither the past nor present had left a damaging effect on me. The constant struggle to make the act and reality match was taking its toll. And at the end of the day, when I was alone with reality and no one saw me, I began to sink into a deep depression.

The truth is — I was scared.

Life in high school had offered simplicity. You were required to be in classes and to attend practices and games. Rules about conduct were spelled out, and those with wisdom and experience made decisions for our academic futures. But life beyond those walls required me to face new situations and make decisions for my own destiny.

That next fall I began attending Olney Central Junior College. I was determined to make myself as involved and as popular as I had been in high school, so I immediately joined the cheerleading squad and began dating one of the baseball players.

My newfound freedom and lifestyle came with a price — responsibility. Responsibility for myself, for my decisions, and for my influence on those I allowed into my life.

I didn't realize it at the time, but I was standing on the same doorsteps my mom had stood on time and again. The lies I told myself about how I was in control and could make better decisions were much stronger than my ability to recognize the troubled path ahead.

Because I hadn't made truth my foundation, I was finding the new stage I was performing on even more demanding and complicated. As my boyfriend and I got closer, there were decisions to be made about intimacy. Having been the victim of molestation as a child, there seemed to be little to consider.

In my mind I had lost my purity long ago, so giving myself freely seemed acceptable and normal.

With that decision, I put on my mask of approval. I told myself this is what love looks like and how it works. But the truth was, because the memories and psychological effects of the molestation were never resolved, I felt dirty after we were together.

For so long it had been okay to deny and sacrifice my emotions for the charade, but with this choice I had sacrificed my heart. I told the inner child who still felt the pain and humiliation of her violation that everything was okay.

While I had been an expert at masking myself for others, it was the first time I had worn the mask for myself, and it was the worst of betrayals.

As the school year progressed, I appeared to have everything under control. I was well liked, a good student, a respected cheerleader, and dating a popular athlete. It seemed as if I had left the ugliness of my past far behind me and had mastered all the emotions that had the potential to bring my performance crashing down.

That false sense of security was shattered when I discovered I was pregnant. Too young to be excited, and too immature to be parents, my boyfriend and I found ourselves hostage to our irresponsibility and angry at each other for the inconvenience. I did what had always outwardly served me well; I immediately put on a mask of indifference for the life we had created. Yet inwardly, my heart churned with the painful memory that I too was a child who was unplanned and unwanted.

Just weeks after the news of my pregnancy, I had a miscarriage. Knowing that the baby wouldn't be subjected to the uncertainties of life was a relief, but there was still a deep sadness that lingered. I was depressed and frustrated, and angry because for the first time I had clearly lost control of my carefully managed life.

With my world and my façade quickly unraveling, I decided I needed a change of scenery. I moved to Houston — determined to get my life back on track. But, Houston wasn't far enough to run from the pain, so I moved back to Olney after only three months.

Returning to college for the summer session, I rejoined the cheerleading squad and resumed my relationship with my boyfriend, although none of it seemed as satisfying as before.

Perhaps losing a child had made me mature and look at things differently, or maybe I was just exhausted from trying to portray a happy life when it was filled with so much pain and contradiction. Regardless, the disguise was no longer working.

That's the problem with masks — even the wearer comes to believe the deceit and then is desperately lost when the façade is finally peeled away. Clearly, if I didn't know who I was, it would be difficult to know who I was supposed to be moving forward.

During that summer I took on several jobs just to keep my mind occupied and one step ahead of the emptiness. One of the jobs was for a family, the Rands, who had an autistic son. That job had significant impact on my life for two very different reasons, and the family's influence and imprint would be evident for many years to come.

It was the first time my life I had developed a connection with a healthy and nurturing family structure. Because of the nature of the work, providing personal and detailed care for their son, I was awarded their confidence and trust for the most complex and delicate details of their lives. In that role, I quickly earned their acceptance and inclusion as family, being treated far more like a daughter than a caregiver.

But it was more than simply being regarded as one of their own — they truly cared about my life's direction and believed in my dreams for the future.

They offered nothing less than whole-hearted support for my success. And because they understood it would be a necessary component to that success, they consistently emphasized that it was okay to ask for and receive help. Perhaps their keen awareness of need and their dedication to nurturing allowed them to recognize and respond to the broken parts of me. Whatever the case, they became the family support I had always longed for, securing a revered and rare place in my heart.

My adopted family – The Rands!

Second, the job required a transparency and vulnerability I had never shared. When I was with their son, he had no expectation of me and no disappointment in me. He just liked me for me and was happy I was there with him.

The experience for me was both liberating and terrifying. Liberating because I discovered the transparency did not actually emphasize my brokenness, but instead allowed me to step beyond it.

But it terrified me to know my heart could undo all my head had taught me about protecting myself and staying in control.

While I would ultimately leave the family's employment

wearing the same masks I arrived with, it was undeniable that the experience made me see myself more clearly and honestly than ever before. I had been given an up-close-and-personal look at the girl in hiding, and the image could not be erased.

Even though I returned to my normal life, it would be impossible to forget the distress and confusion I had seen behind the mask.

After my first year of junior college, my boyfriend left to attend the University of Mississippi. Because he was one of the closest relationships I'd ever had, it was difficult to let him go. We promised each other phone calls and weekend trips to be sure we stayed connected. On one of my trips to see him, I discovered he had been cheating on me, and I promptly ended the relationship.

I was devastated and quickly sank into a depression that would open the door to excessive drinking to dull the pain. But with each episode, when the effects of the alcohol wore off, the grip of loneliness seemed even tighter.

That was the deceit of the alcohol.

The feeling of relief was temporary. Its only real promise was to bring me full circle so I could stare into the face of my despair again and again. And now, with alcohol failing me, too, I found myself desperately wondering how to regain control and outrun the life crumbling around me.

The following year, after graduating from junior college, I moved to Edwardsville to attend Southern Illinois University. I joined the cross-country team and immersed myself in school activities, committees, and fundraisers.

For the first time in a long time my life appeared to be under control again. But as past history had shown, it was just that, an appearance. The smiles, the energy, the enthusiasm: they were all managed distractions to hide the continuing pain and unhappiness. I was still struggling emotionally. I still loathed myself and still hadn't honestly faced my past or my present.

And the drinking and partying was my one assurance that I would never have to.

While living in Edwardsville, I met a neighbor who intrigued me a bit. It was 2000, and I was 20.

His name was Joe.

He was a sweet guy, soft-spoken, and fun, and as neighbors and fellow athletes we saw each other around the complex often. We talked frequently, and I sensed a sincerity and goodness in him that I hadn't come across before. Although I was intrigued with the transparency he demonstrated, I was also completely aware that our worlds were miles apart.

His was a life free of inhibitions and restrictions.

He was everything he professed to be, with no hidden agendas. No pretenses. No games.

On the other hand, mine was a carefully rehearsed orchestration of identities, a collection of masks, and a tightrope act that relied on demanding details, precision, and extreme caution.

Quite honestly I was captivated, even mesmerized by the total freedom I saw in Joe. The ability to unashamedly be yourself and to be comfortable in your own skin seemed like an amazing gift. But for me, that kind of freedom was much like that pony I wished for as a kid.

I wanted it desperately. I dreamed of it, every detail. But as time went on without a pony, I convinced myself to stop wishing and wanting and dreaming, because reality dictated it could never be mine.

Though my interactions with Joe sparked a deep longing for a simpler, freer existence, reality shone a spotlight on all the reasons why it would never be possible. The masks had become an integral part of me. The lies, the personas, the deceptions were details I relied on to get through another day, another month, another year. To lower them now would require painful honesty — both with myself and others.

I couldn't fathom that level of transparency, or the reactions of disbelief and disapproval that were likely to follow once the real me was exposed.

For me, no matter how enticing Joe had made freedom seem, the price of transparency was much too high to pay. As the next few months of my life unfolded, that was the mask I learned to hate the most — pretending my heart didn't ache for the act to be over.

In 2004, I graduated from the university and again found myself losing my audience. For four years my worth had been defined by my athletic achievements and my extracurricular activities, and now I was on my own again, released to find the direction and purpose that had always eluded me. Even Joe, with the exception of helping him make travel arrangements for his honeymoon several years later, would be left as a fond memory in my college years.

After graduation I worked several jobs and lived with two different families, then ultimately on my own. Finding a new rhythm outside of academics and sports was a welcome change, but it didn't take long to realize that the emotional struggles I wrestled with had simply tagged along into this new phase of my life.

It's interesting how a change in scenery or circumstance is said to make life better. When you carry the weight of the years with you, the new will very quickly seem old, and the old will seem even heavier because it is compounded by disappointment. With the disillusionment of the masks compounding daily, I was increasingly more depressed.

One of the jobs I had required that I travel extensively. The frequent business trips were ideal because they helped lessen the void I felt after leaving college and all of my extracurricular activities.

Though it had been difficult to lose the stage I was used to performing on, I quickly found I could be equally convincing in the business world. In all my dealings, I was engaging and impressive, ready to tackle and master whatever the job required. I was confident and successful, and in my meetings I was energetic and unstoppable. There was no question that during the work hours I was solidly in control, but the nights in the hotel rooms told a much different story. It was there in the quiet, when I had no audience, that I was forced to keep company with the real me.

Like an actress stripping away her makeup at the end of a performance, I would sit on the edge of the hotel bed and remove my mask, only to see truth looking back at me in the mirror. Without my mask of confidence, I saw a person who always felt inadequate. A person who was afraid she would never be enough to really matter. Without my painted-on smile, I saw a person whose wounds went so deep that sadness was the only true emotion to be felt. Without my mask of success, I saw a person who never escaped the truth that she was unwanted and seemingly void of any value. But after a drink or two the truth would thankfully begin to fade. I would wake in the morning ready to reapply the masks that had successfully kept the real me concealed for so long.

As time went on, and these quiet moment admissions seeped uninvited into the recesses of my heart, the façade became extremely difficult to maintain. Because I was no longer capable of adequately managing the conflict between charade and reality, and was weary from the effort it required, my dependence on alcohol continued to increase. I found myself on this dangerous familiar road of addiction. This was the same road my mom had taken to mask her own pain and disappointments.

The addiction was only too happy to provide me with one more mask. Denial. Even though my mom and I had arrived at the same destination in life, even though our wounds had led us both to dead ends, I was able to see my situation differently.

For me it wasn't addiction — it was temporary escape

and relief. It wasn't substance abuse — it was a coping mechanism. I followed recklessly in my mom's footsteps but continued to assure myself that I was nothing like her.

How could I be? She didn't have control of her life. But I had mastered mine. Never mind that it wasn't real and I wasn't happy. She was broken, probably beyond repair, but I had picked up all the pieces of my shattered life and moved on. Never mind that the shards kept cutting me with every step, until finally I had become numb to the pain.

Of all the masks that served me, denial was the most damaging, because it had thoroughly convinced me of every self-destructive lie I had ever told myself.

And the greatest lie — *I was nothing like her.*

Then it happened.

One day denial failed me, and I was brought to the lowest point I would ever experience. I had gone out one night and drank very heavily very quickly and became extremely drunk.

At the end of the evening, my friend took me home, making sure I was safely inside before she left. As the night progressed, my drunkenness turned to sickness, and I made my way out the front door into the darkness to get some fresh air. I remember the cool breeze hitting my face, calming the hot flush. I remember my stomach churning and bending over preparing to vomit. I remember groaning and crying, desperate to feel better. Then I remember nothing else until the honking of a car horn woke me up.

It was morning. I blinked my eyes repeatedly, trying to ease in the piercing sunlight. The horn honked again. I covered my ears and squeezed. My head was pounding. I felt stiff and cold. My hair was tangled and damp.

Where was I? As I twisted, I looked to the side and saw bushes and a walkway. I strained to bring my surroundings into focus. The bushes looked familiar, like the ones outside my house. But why was I out here?

I gradually propped myself up on my elbow and looked behind me to see my townhouse, the front door wide open. I had passed out in the yard and had remained there all night.

I was mortified.

No telling how many passersby had seen me sprawled across the lawn. No telling how many comments were made about the drunk who hadn't made it into the house. No telling how many people pointed and laughed at my expense.

As I sat there trying to coordinate my legs with the desire to stand and go inside, I realized I had lost all control. Despite my best efforts to remake and redefine myself, I had been unmasked and exposed in the most humiliating of ways.

In that moment, sitting alone and disheveled in my front yard, I realized my worst fear had come true — *I had become my mom.*

PART IV

The Faith

"Faith is taking the first step
even when you don't see the whole staircase."

~ Martin Luther King, Jr.

11

With Surrender: His Mercy

Exposed and embarrassed, I wiped the drool from the corner of my mouth and attempted to smooth my hair with my trembling hand. I glanced around to see if there were any onlookers, then adjusted the top of my dress and tugged on the hem to cover my thighs. In some odd way I thought if I could make myself appear normal and presentable, I'd be unnoticeable and inconspicuous.

I wasn't.

A few early morning walkers rounded the corner and glanced my way, then quickly back at each other, greeting the day's entertainment with muffled giggles.

I dropped my head in a moment of disgrace. All the years I had successfully kept it together on the outside were disproven and negated in this unplanned display, this spectacle of the woman behind the mask. I closed my eyes to block out the on-lookers' amusement, then took a deep breath, determined to make my way back to the safety and privacy the house offered.

Deep in my heart I knew that any shred of safety or privacy I had been clinging to was no longer mine to keep. I was not just looking at rock bottom, but had fallen into it head first and had all of the wind knocked out of me.

As I finally stood to my feet, my well-managed life now in pieces and unrecognizable, I groaned out loud, "What have I done?"

Instantly, in that place deep in your soul where you can't deny you've heard God speak, He confirmed, "You have become the very thing you despise."

My stomach churned. Not from the hangover, but from the realization that it was true. I was anything but the person I claimed to be.

I had made a tangled mess of my own life, and now had nothing left but desperation. Nothing. No other path to choose, no other façade to hide behind, no ability to control just one more lie. The crushing blow of rock bottom had broken truth wide open and signaled an end to the reality I had defined, created, and manipulated. And the hopelessness and desperation I felt, was like no other I had experienced in my complicated, unbalanced life.

Closing the door behind me, the tears began to flow. I sat down on the sofa, not really knowing what to do with the truth I'd just been handed.

In my childhood experiences I had certainly

encountered desperation, but in those moments my spirit only knew to cry because I felt broken. As an adult, though, the desperation felt much more final, like I was unfixable.

My mind raced wondering what I needed to do next to relieve the despair that now suffocated me. I bowed my head, with my fists pounding my legs I moaned over and over, "What do I do? What do I do?"

In a moment of complete surrender, I dropped my weary shoulders, lifted my head heavenward and said out loud, "I'll do anything."

The word surrender carries a negative connotation, and often stirs resistance in the human heart. Surrender suggests control and domination. Human nature defiantly responds, "You won't get the best of me."

And in that state of stubbornness and determination to do things my way, I was right — no one would get the best of me. Not me. Not God. Not anyone else.

I could never be my best or do my best until I was willing to let God show me who and what that is.

Drying my eyes, I took a deep breath and let it out slowly. The anxiousness of previous moments had given way to an indescribable silence, and an unexpected feeling of relief swept over me.

"Okay God, what now," I asked.

Immediately, again in that place deep in my soul I undeniably heard God speak. I was directed to call the pastor.

Interestingly, throughout the many phases in my life, I had always stayed involved in church. Whenever I moved to new towns for college or work, one of the first things I would do was find a church to attend. Though the life I led behind the masks did not reflect God's values, there was something about the prayer I said as a young girl at my grandmother's house that made me know God was important.

Even though I had not developed a personal, intimate relationship with Him, I clearly understood that He was deserving of recognition, at the very least.

At this point in time I was working with the youth at the church I was attending. When God instructed me to call the pastor, there was a high level of apprehension on my part, for two reasons:

Asking God for help was one thing, but asking people for help was something I was not comfortable with, something I would never do. Asking people was humbling, requiring more vulnerability than I was willing to share.

And, what was I supposed to say? *Hello, pastor. The person you trusted as a role model and spiritual example to the youth in your church has been wearing a disguise all this time.*

How could I ever bring myself to say that?

I sat with my hand on the telephone for several minutes, thinking perhaps I could negotiate with God for a different requirement to satisfy my *I'll do anything* commitment. But God in His wisdom, knowing the necessary steps for the best results, pressed me to call the pastor.

With my head and heart pounding, I dialed the phone number and nervously explained my current state of despair.

Very soon after the call I found myself on the pastor's couch sleeping off a painful hangover. In between periods of sleep, he and his wife fed me crackers and water to address the nausea, all along attending to me with unconditional love.

At each act of kindness, my guilt and shame wanted to shout out, *but I messed up! Don't you get it — I'm unfixable.*

But with each confession my mind devised, my heart was overwhelmed by the judgment-free mercy that was being expressed and shared. I was the greatest of imposters, yet I was being showered with compassion and understanding and forgiveness. With my surrender, God was able to share His mercy. And though it was not clear to me at the time, His mercy was the very thing that would bring out the best in me.

By the time I left the pastor's house, I had vowed to make alcohol a thing of my past, understanding that it had not served me well. With that determination my heart grew increasingly restless about my purpose and life's direction. I think most of my life I had felt unsettled and dissatisfied, but never had a name for it. But now, looking at my life through the compassion and forgiveness God had expressed, it was simply not enough to make life a right foot, left foot experience. I wanted more, but I had no idea what the more was or how to achieve it.

Since I had held a place of leadership with the church youth, the remaining pastoral staff had been advised of my struggle. So when I visited with the worship pastor and his wife several days later, it was a relief that I didn't have to cover or side-step my indiscretions. We talked openly about choices and forgiveness, about God's mercy and second chances, and about my daily walk with sobriety. They ended our visit with one powerful question: "Michelle, what do you want to do with your life?"

I sat speechless for a moment. How could they have known that was the very question that had been stirring in my heart since sobering up? Though I hadn't been able to articulate it up to that moment, the answer to their question was simple: "I want to use my story to help people."

With that confession, and realizing that my dream would require extensive mentoring, the worship pastor and his wife told me about a life coach in Sacramento, California that they wanted me to meet and possibly work with. Without fully understanding the concept of life coaching, but willing to do what was necessary to get my life on track, I agreed, and within just a few weeks I flew him to St. Louis to begin working with me.

Aside from our initial face-to-face meeting, we continued to work together over the phone, but within a few months I knew that in order for the process to really take root I would need to move to Sacramento. Without hesitation, I made plans for the transition.

I arrived in Sacramento on Valentine's Day. As the plane prepared to descend into the airport, the flight attendant instructed us to fasten our seatbelts. Watching the city come into focus below, I remember thinking I also needed to fasten my seatbelt for the unknown that awaited me.

With the exception of the life coach, I knew no one in

Sacramento. I had left a very good job in Illinois and had absolutely no prospects for work in California. If anyone had asked me about my plans or my tomorrows, I would not have been able to answer.

All I knew for sure was that this seemed to be the door that was opening for me to renew my life and discover my purpose.

Because I had no employment, independent living was not an option when I arrived in Sacramento. So I lived with the life coach and his wife for the first three months. During that time I spoke on several occasions with Jason, an associate of the life coach, as well as a pastor of one of the local churches.

There was something genuine and transparent about Jason that I liked and was immediately drawn to. But he was also very inquisitive and direct, and that unnerved me a bit. I had come to Sacramento to start a new life, but I was determined to keep my guard up so that my past couldn't follow me and be uncovered.

It's interesting how moving 1,600 miles from home, to a place I had never seen, to a social network that consisted of three people, was easier than leaving the façade behind. Even though I was embarking on a new life, wearing a disguise was a habit, a survival mechanism that was woven into the fabric of my being. But the fresh start and old habits would soon become adversaries, each bent on an opposing result.

With any personal change and growth, surrender is a key element. Surrender is not just one and done, it is a process. That was a difficult concept for me to understand because I had already humbled myself and asked for help in Illinois; I left the alcohol behind, I said yes to the mentoring program, and yes to the move. In my mind that was the answer to my despair. Period. Problem solved.

When God offers new life, He intends for that life to be exceedingly and abundantly more than we can ask or think. With the pain and dysfunction of my past still lurking behind the mask I brought to Sacramento, the abundance God promised would only be a possibility. It was only through the mercy shown after each challenge, each surrender, that abundance could become a reality.

Little did I know that when I first uttered the words of surrender, *I'll do anything*, God put a plan into motion that would give me opportunities to peel away my carefully guarded persona and reveal the Michelle He intended. Opportunities. Not demands, not commands. Opportunities.

When there is surrender, God is willing to orchestrate prospects that will allow for success. When we seek fulfillment or significance or restoration, God places influential people in our paths and provide moments of decision, so that we can grow and thrive.

Make no mistake; the depth of our growth coincides with our willingness to accept the opportunities He provides. And while all accepted opportunities will move us forward, there will be those that are more difficult and challenging, because they are meant to address the deeper issues and accomplish more.

Much like peeling an onion, we will experience tears with many of the layers, but will also experience great joy once the challenge is completed.

The peeling away of many of my personal layers was connected to Pastor Jason. (Again, the amazing planning that occurred on my behalf: God carefully orchestrating the crossing of our paths through a life coach that a family 1,600 miles away just happened to know.) As I mentioned before, Jason was inquisitive and very direct, a cut-to-the-chase, no-nonsense kind of guy. And given how tightly I guarded my charade, Jason was just the man God needed for the job.

As I continued to work with the life coach, I was determined to take on any challenge or assignment necessary to move my life forward. But the persona I wore – the tough-as-nails, girl-in-control image – didn't set well with Jason during our increasingly frequent interactions.

To him it looked like a counterfeit — a sham.

And at an appointed time, when God knew my heart was ready for the first challenge, He nudged Jason to call me on the disguise I was wearing.

I'll never forget the moment. Jason and I were involved in a conversation that for all intents and purposes should have bothered me, but I maintained my game face, determined to be in control and not flinch. In the middle of the interaction, Jason looked me straight in the eye and demanded, "What's your problem?

I was stunned for a moment. Like a deer in the headlights, there was the initial freeze moment, then the inclination to flee for safety. But I couldn't let him see my gut reaction or the slipping of the mask. So with shoulders thrown back and an imitation confidence, I quipped right back, "There is no problem."

Everything inside of me wanted to burst into tears. He scared me. He was poking at the pieces of me that were off limits, places no one had ever been allowed before. Rather than cry, I stood even straighter, squared off again, and looked him straight in the eye, convinced this time he would buy my display of self-assuredness.

But the façade layer that God was focused on had not yet been peeled back, and Jason assertively countered with, "So what are your issues?"

I swallowed hard.

My bravado was quickly disintegrating, and my secrets felt threatened. This time my shoulders slumped a bit and my knees felt weak, but I still managed an adamant, albeit less convincing, response of, "I don't have any issues."

I don't remember how we ended the conversation, but I do remember I would not surrender in that moment. Later that night, still shaken by the encounter, I knelt beside my bed and laid out new ground rules for God. The wounds of my past were off-limits. What I wanted to accomplish in my life today was not connected to my yesterdays, and I wanted, no, expected, a clean break.

It was a strange demand, given that I wanted to help people with my story. But my concept of helping was simply identifying with their brokenness. I had not yet considered that the story would have little significance without the healing of the brokenness. With the guidelines set, and a quick amen to end the discussion, I climbed into bed ready to leave the events of the day behind.

Instead, I tossed and turned all night, Jason's intrusive question burning a hole in my secretly damaged, well-guarded heart.

From that time on I decided my association with Jason would be strictly business. Pleasantries and exchanges within the boundaries of life-coaching interactions were fine, but heart-revealing conversations were barred and no longer fair game. But as determined as I was to avoid his curiosity and probing, there was a part of me that kept wondering what else he knew about me. Oddly enough, when Jason shed light on the woman behind the mask, there was a sense of relief.

I was weary from carrying the secrets for so long, and that momentary exposure almost felt like a respite from the weight. I felt extremely conflicted; wanting to hide, but imagining what it would be like to step out of the shadows.

I didn't understand it then, but God had started a work within me and was preparing to remove a layer that would begin to disassemble my façade. Despite my insistence that He leave my secrets intact and my past behind, God continued to create opportunities for transparency with Jason.

What I determined would be "just business," turned out to be exactly that, but it was God's business – His plan to restore and reinvent my life. And Jason was the divinely appointed, best choice to touch my heart and begin to loosen the layers.

On a number of occasions the work I was doing with my life coach found me in Jason's home sharing conversations with him and his wife, Lynette. From one visit to the next, as we became better acquainted and Jason's approach seemed less intrusive, I found myself slowly allowing them to peer into the dysfunction that had followed me to California.

I was still guarded — exposing just enough for them to understand where I was coming from, without surrendering my control or expressing my need for change. It was restricted openness; the level of sharing was at my discretion, and my ability to leave whenever the topic became too uncomfortable was my decision. Even when a conversation did touch a nerve and leave me feeling uncomfortable, I would drive away from their home secretly longing for the next visit.

Looking back, I understand now that my scarred and sheltered heart was being drawn to God's intended work, to the healing process that He offered in compassion, understanding, and forgiveness.

After living with the life coach and his wife for three months, I felt the need to move on.

I had no adequate means to rent an apartment or live on my own, and a sparse supply of friends to impose upon. Nevertheless, I packed my car with all my belongings and watched the past months' shelter grow smaller in the rear view mirror.

I sighed heavily. I was now homeless.

But God had already begun to orchestrate a plan on my behalf, and in His wisdom was about to present me with an astonishing opportunity. The opportunity, however, would be paired with the very difficult and frightening requirement of ultimate surrender.

Aware that I had moved out of the life coach's house that morning, Jason suggested that I stay with his family for the night. I was flying out the next morning to attend a youth camp associated with my previous church in Illinois, so I thought a night's lodging would be perfect. Then I could decide where I would live once I returned to Sacramento.

That afternoon, Jason, Lynette, and I were sitting in the living room having a casual conversation, when the tone suddenly turned more serious and they asked if they could share their hearts with me. I swallowed hard. "Sure", I said apprehensively.

Then Jason called to the children, asking them to come in and join the family discussion. My heart raced and my hands began to tremble. My mind was preparing me for the possibility that they had reconsidered the evening's accommodations, and I began to imagine having to pick up my overnight bag and drive alone into homelessness.

After the children got settled on the sofa, Jason began to explain that after much prayer and discussion, he and Lynette wanted me to come live with them and their children, and to be a part of their family. I sat speechless, looking at each face to see if what I was hearing was the truth. And I realized it must have been, because they all stared at me quietly and intently waiting for my response to the proposition.

I wanted to pinch myself.

I was elated and mortified all at the same time. If I accepted their offer, I would have something I'd always imagined — a home. But I was also aware that God meant business about addressing my past and authenticity.

Surrendering my disguise would be the prerequisite, and retreating when discussions got tough and exposure was threatened would not be an option. As unsettling as that prospect was, I somehow knew that the mercy that brought me to Sacramento, would be the same mercy that would see me through this terrifying, but divinely appointed step. So in 2007, I agreed to the offer and whole-heartedly surrendered to give God the chance to uncover and reveal the best of me.

12

With Vulnerability: His Grace

I was 27-years-old when I moved in with Jason's family. It was a mild day in May, and as I walked to my car to retrieve my belongings, I was captivated once again by the surrounding beauty. Their home was located in the foothills outside of Sacramento. It was secluded and peaceful, a wide-open lot with trees and wild grass.

Since the first time I visited Jason and Lynette, I was enamored with the property, because it reminded me of a little piece of heaven. Even though I had known it was time to leave the Midwest months earlier, I was a small-town girl at heart, and I missed the country feel I was used to. Now, I just couldn't believe God had responded to my heart's longing and given me a piece of home in Northern California.

When I reached for the car door, a cool gust of wind brushed my face. And with it, an immediate barrage of questions and concerns flooded my mind. *Would I feel comfortable here? Would I fit in? Would I really be considered family? Would they change their minds once I'd been here a while?*

I gripped the car door handle a little tighter, a lump settling in my throat. Suddenly the idea of belonging carried more angst than excitement, and the reality of committing to the unknown began to rouse second thoughts. But because I had already surrendered to God's apparent plan for this next phase of my life, I told myself there was no turning back now.

Standing on the front porch I took a deep breath, my hand trembling as I pushed the door open into the entryway. Within just minutes of their offer, I was crossing the threshold of Pastor Jason's home carrying all of my baggage and two suitcases. I was excitedly welcomed by the children as I stepped into the living room, then after a brief expression of thankfulness for their hospitality, was escorted to the guest room to get settled.

I unpacked slowly, taking great care to organize my belongings on the nightstand and in the dresser drawers. Pushing the final drawer closed, I looked up and into the mirror. I stared at myself intently for a moment, trying to wrap my head around the enormity of this gift and wondering how I was even deserving. Then I began to focus on the reflection of the warmth and safety that surrounded me, and I understood that by God's grace alone, by His free and unmerited favor, I was standing in the place He had prepared just for me, for this very moment in my life.

As I was storing the empty suitcases in the back of the closet, the sounds of family life drifted down the hall. I heard the children talking simultaneously to their dad about events of their day, and Lynette announcing plans for dinner.

I sat on the edge of the bed and smiled to myself. This was the family, the enthusiasm, the love and laughter, I was invited to be a part of. Looking around the cozy room I would now call home, I felt incredibly grateful. Intrigued by the sounds of the home, and confident in my ability to adapt, I had a comforting thought that maybe surrender wasn't going to be that difficult after all.

What I didn't understand was my surrender was just the beginning of the healing and restoration process I had embarked on. It wasn't about the clothes hung neatly in the closet or my Bible laying impressively on the shelf. It was about the decades of baggage that I had brought into the room with me. The baggage I was ready to pretend wasn't there.

It was easy to do – I'd been doing it all my life. But in this new setting I would soon learn that it would not be allowed, and vulnerability would be the next sacrifice I would be required to make for true restoration to occur.

Vulnerability means being susceptible to being wounded, to being hurt, to being open or exposed to criticism. If I'd been asked beforehand, neither form of vulnerability would have been acceptable to me, but both were poised to play a significant part in the life lessons I was about to learn. On many occasions the fearful child-like spirit that hid deep inside me would be the one exposed and challenged, and on other occasions, the 27 year-old woman would simply be called into account.

Unknowingly, I had begun the process of God blending the parts of me that had been separated for so long into a whole and complete individual.

As human nature dictates, my moments of vulnerability were often met with embarrassment, and frustration.

And sometimes fear.

It reminded me of movies I'd seen where guns were pointed at the good guys and their hands were raised to signal surrender. Then they were told to get on their knees, immediately becoming vulnerable to the mercy of another.

While I understood in my heart that God would not harm me in the growth process He initiated, there was still a part of me that questioned why being vulnerable was a condition. But I would quickly learn that while surrender was the acceptance of healing, vulnerability, acknowledged and expressed, would bring progress in my healing.

Looking back now I can honestly say that through the exposure of my vulnerabilities came my greatest emotional and spiritual development.

Lynette kept an amazing home. It was well-organized, orderly, simply yet beautifully decorated, and above all, warm and inviting. The atmosphere was comfortable and tranquil, with pleasant conversations around the family dinner table; laughter shared when stories were told, and a genuine enjoyment of each other's company.

To her, a balanced home was as important as a balanced checkbook, understanding that every act of kindness was an investment in the physical, emotional, and spiritual well being of the family.

Their home was a sanctuary, a safe haven that intrigued and captivated my heart.

As welcomed as I was in their home, and as wonderful as the harmony and camaraderie felt, there was a piece of baggage I carried that kept me from fully immersing myself in the freedom of the environment. It's interesting that when you surrender to God, He will place you in situations that stir memories and emotions of the past that restrict us in our present. When allowed, that stirring opens the door to the vulnerability needed to address and resolve past issues, so that we can approach the future with liberty and hope.

For me the baggage was fear; fear of abandonment, instability, and disappointment. I had packed the bag when I was a child, and carried it quietly and privately into adulthood.

My present situation posed no looming threat of any of those things, but the bruised little girl in me feared the worst and planned accordingly. Evidenced by the tiny portions of food I took at mealtimes, I was fearful that if I ate too much Jason and Lynette wouldn't want me to stay. It seems silly to admit now, but the memory of being hungry at Sue's and my desperate desire not to be a burden had crippled my ability to receive the generosity and safety being offered by this loving and accepting family.

Several weeks after moving in, another situation prompted the same feelings of fear. I was in the shower, and while shaving my legs, placed my foot on the soap tray on the wall. Suddenly the tray ripped away from the wall and fell forcefully into the spiraling water at the bottom of the tub.

I was mortified.

I don't even remember if I finished rinsing off the soap, but I do remember my breath leaving me for fear of the consequences.

I started to cry.

Jason's family had opened their beautiful home to me, and I had broken something in it. Not on purpose, but still, I was the cause of the damage. I left the bathroom, the soap tray wrapped tightly in an extra towel, and walked hurriedly to my room. My heart was pounding and my hands trembling as I pulled out a piece of paper and wrote a tearful apology note for my carelessness. I dressed slowly that morning, waiting for everyone to leave the house so I could place the soap tray and apology note on the kitchen counter for discovery later that day.

More baggage.

Memories of a little girl not getting it right and being too much trouble rested heavy on my shoulders that day. Because those messages had so entangled my damaged heart, I expected my presence in the home to now be seen as a problem, and was convinced I would be asked to leave and lose the opportunity to be part of a family.

I could barely focus on work anticipating the consequence that awaited me. I drove to the house slowly that evening. When I arrived and stepped into the kitchen, the soap dish and note were still laying on the counter. The family was engaged in the usual banter as they prepared the dinner meal. I looked at Jason for some sort of reaction. I was prepared, ready for the consequence. But he just looked at me, smiled, and continued his exchange with the children. *Hadn't they seen this?*

I quickly looked at Lynette, thinking maybe she was the one who would deal with the issue. But she too acknowledged me with a nod and a smile.

Finally, with a lull in the family's conversation, I blurted out, "Jason, I'm really sorry about the soap dish. I didn't mean to break it."

Leaning with his back against the counter he looked at me and nonchalantly responded, "It's okay, we'll fix it", then returned his attention to the kid's conversation.

I was dumbfounded. *That was it? No request to leave, no reprimand, no expression of disapproval?*

Though my heart was confused in that moment, I later understood that God was displaying forgiveness and acceptance in a most practical way. He had brought me into a loving home to show me His purpose and plan for family. With my heart surrendered and my vulnerability laid bare, He demonstrated that day that I no longer needed to fear the instability that had wounded me so deeply.

I could rely on the security and safety that was always meant to be mine.

Without question, the lesson I learned from the soap dish healed something deep inside and helped me relax into the family dynamic. I enjoyed spending time with the kids, making brownies, playing games, putting puzzles together, and making an odd frozen pickle concoction I called pickle-sicles.

As time went on, nine-year-old Maddie and I argued like sisters over hairbrushes and kitchen duty. And Jason's son, seven-year-old Siah, and I established a routine of brushing our teeth together every night before bedtime prayers — an activity in which I was required to be an active participant.

Even though I had found safety within the family and enjoyed more freedom in my spirit, there was still lingering baggage that needed to be removed from my heart if I were to experience the fullness of healing God intended. But with the next challenge, both the little girl and 27-year-old woman in me had a hand on the bag, making vulnerability a bit more complicated.

Jason approached me privately one day and invited me to my first, "Sit down, let's talk" conversation. Very directly, but kindly, Jason informed me that one of my behaviors wasn't fitting in with the household guidelines.

My mind raced. *I've been helpful and courteous; I've been pleasant and respectful.*

I sat bewildered, much like a kid who knows she's in trouble but is oblivious to the why.

"It's about your bedtime," he said matter-of-factly, "it's not going to work within our family structure."

Wait. What? My sleep schedule seemed like an odd thing to address. I didn't disturb anyone when I watched TV late at night, and tried not to be disruptive when I got up early for a morning run. I felt a bit irritated. I was a grown woman and I was being spoken to about my bedtime. This was just me. It was the way I'd always lived, making up my own rules, and keeping my own hours.

I slumped back in the chair to give an obligatory listen to the expectations of my host. Quite frankly, as Jason began explaining how families have schedules and those schedules contribute to the order of the household, I felt both embarrassed and defensive.

Embarrassed, because as he explained it, it seemed like something I should have known as an adult; and defensive because my baggage of an unorthodox upbringing was being pulled out of the shadows, placed on the table, and I was being told to look at it honestly. I didn't like it, but the more Jason explained the reasons, the more receptive I felt to the message.

All those years I had been dragging the kid in me along by the wrist, insisting she live like me, without order or boundaries. Suddenly I pictured her weary and worn, and felt ashamed that I had never allowed her to feel the security that comes from expectations and responsible behavior.

Once again, God in His grace allowed the home He placed me in to reveal a truth that would further liberate my spirt.

In that moment, Jason served as a father figure, thoughtfully explaining his genuine concern for my best interest and well-being. It was something I'd never experienced before, and my willingness to be vulnerable to his instruction and receptive to the concept of order would guarantee another piece of baggage would be removed from my journey.

Not surprisingly, it was easier for me to rescue the little girl inside than it was to reinvent the adult I had become over the years. Even though I had developed a deep love for the security of this home and family life, the broken 27-year-old still struggled with an informal attitude brought about by an unstructured past. It was a piece of my baggage that proved difficult to pry from my hand.

That challenge became apparent one evening when I strolled in significantly late from work to find the family already sitting down to the dinner meal. I casually sat my purse on the counter and pulled out my designated chair.

"You're late," Jason said firmly, his stare unbroken. My face felt flushed as all eyes were on me. Spreading my napkin on my lap I made my mouth say "sorry", but inside my head I was countering with, *yeah, so what's the problem?*

"If it's not planned, it's not acceptable," he continued. Out of the corner of my eye I saw the kid's heads snap my direction to catch my reaction.

"Understood," I said apologetically. But I truly didn't understand. And throughout the remainder of the meal my mind kept pondering, *what's the big deal?*

As soon as the dishes were cleared and the children were

off to their homework, Jason called me into the living room. By all appearances, it was going to be another of his "sit down, let's talk" conversations. I was hoping my dinnertime apology had covered my indiscretion, but it was apparent there was more to this admonition.

"Do you understand why it's important, Michelle?" he asked softly. My eyes scanned the room, as if the answer was conspicuously lying on a shelf.

"I think so," I said, without really having a clue.

"It's because people depend on you," he revealed. My mind shifted into high gear. *Depend on me! Hold on. I never signed up for that. I have my hands full just being responsible for myself.*

Jason went on to explain that whether it be God, family, work, ministry, or friendships, it was important to recognize the value of reliability. If you are expected to be somewhere, be there early. If you committed to a task, give it your all. If you give your word, never let it betray you. Dependability, he concluded, speaks to your character, to the value of others, and leaves an impression that's not quickly forgotten.

After an abbreviated bedtime prayer that night, I slipped under the covers ready to put the evening behind me. But I was still frustrated by what Jason had said, and the more I thought about it, the more reprimanded and defensive I felt. For several minutes I stared silently at the ceiling while tears filled and burned my eyes. Like a pressure cooker, I released a pent up breath and issued a challenge to God to provide an explanation for Jason's unreasonable reaction.

"What's the big deal? I was late for dinner. Seriously, God, do you get it?" I muttered in a somewhat demanding tone. "This idea of people being affected by me is absurd. I never had anyone to rely on, and I'm fine."

In that instant, my words convicted me.

I wasn't fine.

The broken kid in me knew it, and deep down, so did the woman lying there with the tear-drenched face. It was undisputable I had mastered the art of self-reliance — depending on no one, independent and proud. As my head rested on my tear-soaked pillow, I felt the weight of all my exhaustion from a long solitary journey. This idea of others relying on me when I myself had no one to rely on was terribly unsettling.

Picturing that moment now, I understand God and I were in that room negotiating the surrender of my baggage of self-reliance. The issue was really not about me being relied upon by others, it was about me being willing to rely on God. I was being asked to release my grip, and to become God-reliant in order to experience another level of healing.

He wanted to rescue me from the weight of going it alone, and give me the opportunity to find Him reliable and dependable in all the growth and changes that were still ahead. It was a surrender I had never considered before, and a truth I would be required to accept before I could move forward effectively.

I was in a moment of decision.

It was as if the bed was a neutral zone, and in the morning I would have to decide which side to get out on.

One side represented permission to let God continue His work of restoration. True, the work to that point had been challenging, and I had been required to be uncomfortably vulnerable, but I had never been disappointed in the outcome, and He had always richly blessed my willingness and efforts.

The other side represented the ability to stand my ground and draw a line that He had asked too much. It was the right to plant my feet and declare a stopping point in His expectations for my growth. But having experienced the amazing progress He had orchestrated in my life so far, the thought of digging my heels in was nothing less than alarming.

Throughout the night I was restless, finding only a few hours of sleep toward the early morning. Switching off the alarm I laid still for several minutes, rubbing my swollen eyes and weighing the decision before me.

Would I receive Jason's counsel, understanding that his words were a reflection of God's desire to remove another layer of my past and brokenness?

Or would I stop His work mid-way?

The tears began to well up again.

"I'm scared, God," I whimpered, "but I want Your best for me."

From that day on I purposed to be receptive to God's work in my life, and to be reliant on Him for the execution of that work. I'm not saying it was easy, or that there weren't moments when I argued with His methods. It was like a kid with a nasty cut on their knee. When the wound is initially bandaged, the kid often tries to brush away the healing hand with an impassioned plea, "Don't touch it!" Then when the bandage is to be replaced by a clean one, the child often whines and covers the wound with their hand, assuming the pain will be as great the second time as it was the first. Like the cut beneath a bandage, there are multiple stages and reactions to healing, and I experienced all of them. But God in His mercy, in His unmerited favor toward me, was patient and dependable at all times.

As I learned to be more welcoming of my spiritual growth spurts, Jason began to realize that while the adult me was learning to receive and respond to God's guidance, the little girl in me, the one with the broken past, had not yet experienced her own healing.

You see, the point of our deepest wounds in life is usually the place we get stuck emotionally. With abandonment and insecurity as my history, there were emotional gaps to be filled before the wounded child and the woman moving forward could be united. It wasn't just about the portrayal of healing, it was about *being* healed and journeying as a whole and restored person.

With that goal in mind, Jason and I embarked on a memory reset challenge, creating a road map of my complicated young life and identifying where that road had taken me emotionally. Then we began to evaluate the life lessons I'd learned on those twisted paths, and compared those beliefs against the truths in God's word.

I was absolutely astounded by what I learned of my value and significance. And while I appreciated the facts and certainties I had uncovered, I was convinced there was no way to make up for the loving expressions and experiences my wounded child had been denied over the years.

But that's the amazing thing about God.

If He is allowed to heal, He will heal completely. If He is allowed to restore, He will fill in the gaps that have left us hollow, and will satisfy the deepest longings of our hearts.

There were many events God used as healing moments during the three years I spent in Jason and Lynette's home. None were more powerful than the day Jason asked me to start work a bit later, because he had something he wanted me to do. It was the first day of school and we all sat down to breakfast together. The table was lively with conversations about new teachers and old friends, and Lynette reminding the kids of their rules of conduct: first time obey and others first.

After we finished cleaning up the breakfast dishes, the kids excitedly grabbed their backpacks, Lynette handed out lunches, and Jason jingled his keys with a "come on, let's go." I was ready to give the kids some words of praise about how proud I was of them, when Jason said, "You too."

Wait. What?

"Let's go," he said excitedly, "I want you to know what it's like for parents to take their kids to the first day of school."

Overwhelmed with emotion, I threw on a sweatshirt and piled into the car with the family. I'd never done this before, as evidenced by the butterflies in my stomach and the giddiness I felt.

Nudging the kids, I kept asking enthusiastically, "Are you ready?"

But I may as well have been asking myself, because I could barely wait until we reached our destination. Once we got to the school, we took pictures with the kids, Jason urging us to "get closer...now smile."

The atmosphere was amazing; the energy and anticipation made me feel like a kid myself. Then hearing the bell ring, we excitedly walked the kids to their classrooms, Jason and Lynette giving them a kiss and a final wish to have a good day before the door closed behind them.

For the rest of the day, those images kept crossing my mind and stirred up such a peace in my heart. *I had experienced the first day of school with parents.* I may have done it as an adult, but I was keenly aware that the opportunity had been orchestrated for the sole purpose of healing the kid in me.

God, as only He can do, was filling a gap and giving a meaningful moment I'd missed years ago, back to me.

Many other gaps were filled while living with the family. There were Christmas cards with me in the family picture; total acceptance for a girl who never belonged. The routine of family meals, Bible devotions, and bedtime prayers; security for a girl who always felt detached. Brightly decorated birthday celebrations, banners and balloons declaring the significance of the recipient; a loving expression for a girl who never felt special. And though these expressions were powerful in ministering to my little girl heart, there was a special healing that occurred as I watched the daily family dynamics, specifically the hearts of the parents toward the children.

Siah, Jason's son, 20 years my junior, was the life of the party. He had a confidence that was mesmerizing, and an ability to just be himself. Jason frequently challenged us all to be the best version of ourselves, and it was obvious that Siah had accomplished that through the simple acceptance of the challenge.

I remember wishing it could be that easy for me, but I reminded myself that he and I came from very different backgrounds, and that I had spent a lifetime trying to conceal mine. But in being himself, there was an ease and lightness of spirit that was enviable.

As I mentioned earlier, one of our regular routines before bed was to brush our teeth together. Every night over the sink we would talk, and he would ask questions and offer thoughtful responses to my answers. Of course, having spent years feeling self-conscious about my smile, I tended to be a bit shy and guarded when we first started the ritual. But every night as we looked at each other's reflections in the mirror, with toothpaste froth lining his mouth, and his uninhibited swish and spit, God was showing me that our greatest freedom comes from being the person He created, unapologetic and unencumbered by what others might think.

It's funny to realize that such a significant lesson came from a basic daily routine, but sometimes God uses the simplest examples to illustrate His greatest truths. And while I never indulged in a froth-lined mouth, I had begun to understand the freedom of being myself, and not allowing my past to conceal the person God intended.

Maddie, Jason's daughter, 18 years my junior, was affectionately known as my "mini-me". She was blonde and petite, and was always energetic and spirited. We did chores together, battled to be first in line for Drumstick ice creams, had disagreements, giggled about boys, shared confidences, and developed a bond as close as sisters.

As part of the family experience, I observed as she received acceptance and support, as well as counsel and discipline from her parents. I watched as they had discussions and conflicts, and saw the love and wisdom that Jason and Lynette imparted in their explanations and resolutions.

One day in particular I sat quietly and studied a joyful exchange between the three of them, and I was moved by the genuine adoration they expressed for one another. Jason and Lynette had done a wonderful job parenting the children, and my "mini-me" was a beautiful result of their devotion.

My "mini-me!" Suddenly the phrase grabbed my attention. That was it! That's why God brought me here. So I could see the replica of me being cared for and loved in the way God intended. I felt like I couldn't breathe; that feeling you get when someone shares astounding news.

It was by far the most amazing revelation God had bestowed in this season of surrender and vulnerability. Not only was I watching Maddie develop and grow, but through each of those moments, God was imparting understanding and confidence through the compassion and commitment I was witnessing. By allowing me to be an intimate observer of life as it should have been, He was healing the brokenness that had scarred my innocent and impressionable heart.

I bowed my head in extreme gratitude, completely aware that only a God who loves very deeply would be that concerned with every detail of the healing process.

In a sense I was one of the kids, too, and was gently parented right along with them. In addition to the moments Jason spent mentoring me, there were also wonderful growth moments with Lynette.

She and I would spend hours sharing long talks, tears, and prayers. Even in the non-stop role of wife and mother, she always made a safe place for me to share and feel protected. She also taught me about household budgets and family traditions, an amazing investment of time in a girl who never learned about family structures or the complexities and joys of doing life together.

Lynette was full of wisdom. One of the most invaluable lessons I gleaned during my stay was that of good judgement. Whenever a choice was emerging, she would always require the kids and me to consider the "why" of our actions and decisions. We couldn't simply make a decision, but were asked to consider the basis for our choice, and to weigh the benefits and consequences of our actions.

It was a matter of accountability; understanding that we are accountable to both God and to those who love us. Because the majority of my life had required very little accountability, it was a foreign concept, to be sure. But if the result was this well-managed, emotionally healthy, thriving family, then I knew it was something God had put His blessing upon.

For me, that's all that mattered.

The time spent in Jason and Lynette's home was some of the most significant, because it is where I was allowed to experience life in its fullest through surrender and vulnerability. God in His mercy and grace had given me a safe place to grow, and nurtured me constantly through the watchful care of my dear friends. He attended to every aspect of the growth process. From the most inconsequential to the largest detail, He orchestrated the healing and wholeness that had eluded me for so long.

The measure of how much I had grown was demonstrated on two occasions when Maddie came into my room. One day she noticed the Bible on my bed and picked it up, puzzled by the imprint of the front. It read: "Michelle Princess of God".

Quizzing, she asked why my last name was not inscribed. I told her that my last name didn't really matter. What mattered was that God had claimed me, and that was all I needed to be confident of. Those words were a wonderful proclamation that my past could no longer define me, and that God had redeemed what was lost for His glory and my renewal.

The second clear indication of growth occurred when Maddie came into my room with my elementary school yearbooks in her hand. She was troubled that she hadn't been able to find me in their pages. I explained that I went by different last names in school, and when I revealed the name for each year, she turned the pages to find my face scratched off of each one.

When I looked into her perplexed eyes, it was painful to tell her I had once been ashamed of that little girl. And now looking at the scratch marks across each picture, it was the first time ever I regretted that I had abandoned her.

My words that night served as an admission that I now understood my value. With tears in my eyes, I leaned over and hugged my "mini-me." Feeling her sadness for my life, I was able to comfort her with the truth that God rescued my broken heart and gave me a second chance of hope and promise.

The scratched off faces in my Grade School yearbook photos.

For many years my life had resembled a scattered jigsaw puzzle, much like the ones Maddie, Siah and I put together on family nights. Through that activity, God shared two important details about the healing process.

He revealed that I couldn't complete a puzzle if I hold on to the pieces.

In order to see the intended picture, I had to surrender them one by one. Just as I had decided time and again to surrender to God's plan and process for restoration.

He also revealed that I couldn't put a puzzle together all at once.

It must be assembled a piece at a time, and I must be vulnerable enough to share with others and receive new truths and perspectives — just as I had been willing to learn the many life-lessons expressed through the family's love and patience.

It was an awesome revelation, and a wonderful reminder of God's devotion toward me. For all the pieces I had surrendered, He had lovingly reciprocated by unfolding a beautiful picture my life was intended to be. And as He continued to bring unmatched contentment and rest to my heart, I knew He was redeeming my life, piece by piece.

13

With Determination: His Restoration

While living with Jason and Lynette, I entered a discipleship program at the church where Jason served as the outreach pastor. It was exciting to pour myself into something meaningful, and as the months passed, it seemed my passion for the underserved in our church and the Sacramento community began to grow.

At first, my connection with those who were marginalized was simply based on my understanding of where they were coming from. These were people who felt like they didn't belong; I understood that, because for years I walked with that pain. They felt alone and insignificant — I related, because I too had experienced that despair.

What was developing in my heart was not simply a "connection" with the feelings of the hopeless, it was God unwrapping and exposing the "calling" He had placed on my life. He was orchestrating something good to come out of every struggle that had defined my past.

That's the amazing thing about God, He uses everything we are or previously have been to reveal His desire and plan to restore. We don't have to polish our past or our present to make it respectable. We don't have to provide explanations or prepare excuses. We simply come, and allow Him to create beauty from ashes. With that as our desire, brokenness can be re-purposed and our lives can serve as a testament of hope to those who walk a similar path.

As described in Psalm 84:6, I had walked through the valley of weeping, I had dug deep wells in my despair, and He was preparing springs of blessing and encouragement for those I would accompany on their journey to healing and restoration.

Soon after God ignited that spark of compassion for the underserved, an internship position opened up in the outreach department with Jason. I jumped on it. Even though it meant long hours, involvement in multiple programs, and only a $50 a week gas allowance, I believed God had opened the door for me to pursue my passion of helping others.

With my acceptance of the position came my whole-hearted commitment to the task, and a determination to prove myself capable. But in the same way that my healing process had revealed there was more to surrender and more vulnerability than I anticipated, I soon learned that my perception of determination would also be challenged.

The survival instincts I had developed throughout my life created a certain drive within me. I had met difficulties and challenges head-on. In the face of adversity I had risen to the occasion, and I considered myself stronger and wiser for having experienced and endured those situations. It was my determination that had preserved my life and brought me this far.

I was extremely proud of that attribute, and in my mind, it was the best way I knew to prove myself valuable to God.

Determination is defined two ways: it can be a quality that makes you continue trying to do or achieve something that is difficult, or it can be the act of finally deciding something. My definition was the first of the two. I was unwavering in my decision to "show" God He could count on me. But in the arena of life, as well as ministry, trying to do God's work for Him is a precursor to frustration and discouragement.

My flawed understanding of determination was clearly demonstrated one day on the streets of San Francisco. I had gone on a sight-seeing trip with the Rands, the family from Illinois with the autistic son I had worked for years earlier. They were visiting California, and I had mistakenly worn high heels for the day's excursion. For hours we climbed and descended the steep streets.

My feet were killing me, but I was determined not to let anyone know. Soon my strides got shorter, my knees bent more with each step, as I was trying to ease the contact between the sidewalk and my soles.

I was in excruciating pain, but I suffered in silence, determined I could go the distance.

Soon, though, the grimace on my face clued my friends in on my discomfort, and they tried to convince me multiple times that we should find a store so I could buy a pair of walking shoes. But I wouldn't hear of it. I had embarked on this excursion feeling taller, slimmer, and prettier in my heels, and I would conclude in the same attire. In my eyes, anything less would be personal failure and an embarrassment.

When I got home that night, I could hardly pull the shoes off my swollen, blistered feet. I laid on the bed, my legs and feet throbbing from my determination to prove myself. I had certainly faced the challenge my way, but what I valued as determination was really just another piece of baggage I had learned to take great pride in. I can handle it! I can make this work! I can survive! "I can" had become my motto.

I sighed heavily.

These were the very friends who had tried to teach me that it was okay to ask for and receive help. What was I thinking? I had endured hours of unnecessary pain and discomfort all for the sake of saying "I can."

Instead I should have listened to my friends and their wisdom and willingness to help in the situation. Whether it was pride, stubbornness, or arrogance, something inside of me had silenced their voices of reason and assistance. The situation was solely about me, and what I could accomplish. And while I had earned the right to lie there in pain and celebrate my victory, I had to admit that my misguided determination had ultimately hampered the sightseeing experience.

Too uncomfortable to sleep that night, my mind continued to deliberate as I tossed and turned. *Why am I like this? I want to be my best, especially for you God. What am I doing wrong?*

In a sense I felt like Jacob wrestling with the angel. As had been the case in previous growth experiences, I knew there was something in that moment I was meant to understand about myself. Frustrated, I closed my eyes and began a sales pitch of how I could do better if He gave me the chance. "I can, God. I promise," I insisted out loud.

With that statement, my eyes flew open. That was it. That's what He wanted me to understand. The determination I wanted to give, in life as well as ministry, was not what He needed. I was not required to serve Him in my own strength, but was called to walk in His.

The San Francisco trip was a painful illustration of my pride in accomplishing things on my own, and in my own way. I suddenly realized that in the same manner my determination discounted the wisdom of my friends on those steep hills, it was threatening to muffle God's voice and guidance in my life. With my heart drawn toward ministry, that characteristic would only minimize the opportunities and experiences He had planned for me.

Immediately my aching feet became synonymous with the years worth of damage in my spirit. The pain I carried both physically and emotionally was unnecessary and unfortunate, but with the proper care, the pain would lessen and dissipate. For the first time, I understood there was no more need to prove my worth to God.

He had chosen me.

Me.

A broken and damaged girl chosen to experience His restoration and complete freedom of both mind and spirit.

It wasn't about me working for Him — it was about Him working through me. But my determination had to change. Rather than being a trait of continually striving to achieve the impossible, it had to be an action of finally deciding that my value, my worth, my purpose, was established by Him alone.

In the quietness of that long night, that truth became my determination and my prayer. With a tearful "amen" it felt like an incredible weight had lifted from my body. For the first time ever I was free of self-imposed expectations.

The measuring stick I had carried all my life had been broken in two, and was no longer able to minimize the value and potential God had assigned to me.

As I unreservedly placed the pieces in His hands that night, it became more than just a turning point in my heart. It was the beginning of God revealing the essence and potential of effective, life-changing ministry. My passion to reach the disenfranchised had now been fanned from spark to flame, and I was excited to see how God would use my life, my story, to bring change and healing to others who were broken.

With my calling clearly defined, and my source of strength now solidly understood and established, God brought amazing opportunities across my path. And with each opportunity came the potential for more growth and understanding, all meant to enhance and better express my life's purpose.

As the opportunities unfolded, I was constantly amazed at how the path I walked paralleled with the needs of those I was coming in contact with, and I was equally thankful that the transformation in my journey could be an example of the freedom meant for theirs. There was simply no denying that God was fulfilling His promise to bring something good from my broken past and experiences, and that those who were rescued and changed by the power of His love would someday declare the same.

One of the first organizations I got involved with was Be Change, a non-profit organization, founded by Jason and endorsed by the church, working to secure an equal education for inner-city children.

Be Change strives to raise the academic performance of every child in their sponsor schools, by providing for their physical, nutritional, and health care needs. To that end, Be Change supporters participate in marathons throughout the year to raise the funds necessary to subsidize these services.

The first school I was introduced to through Be Change was Oak Ridge Elementary, located in a poor and underserved neighborhood in Sacramento.

Having been on the track team during my middle school and high school years, I was anxious to participate in my first marathon representing Be Change: Run for a Reason.

Jason had set up an 18-week training program to make sure that all the runners were in top physical shape to participate, and I was ready and excited for the challenge. What awaited me through the training process would prepare me not only physically, but spiritually as well. And with my heart having learned much about being vulnerable and receptive, I was determined to listen to all God wanted to teach me in this setting.

When we first started training, I was all about the speed. I was naturally competitive, and in my mind the finish line was the ultimate goal. Jason observed me for the first few sessions, then pulled me aside one day and asked me to reconsider my focus.

It wasn't about the finish line, he shared — it was about each step that made the destination possible. Aware of the calling I felt on my life, Jason explained that if I wanted to be a leader, it should never be about getting to the finish line the fastest, it should be about coming along side those on the same path to encourage and motivate them in their pursuit.

Jason demonstrated this philosophy within our pace groups. Although each group, depending on their fitness level and stamina, moved at a different speed, we all had the same "impact" plan. Once the fastest group completed the course, they would double back and meet the group who was trailing behind and accompany them to the end of the course. Then the combined groups would double back and repeat the process with all the remaining groups.

It was a foreign concept to me, and while the idea of

"impact" was admirable, the importance of the action had not yet fully birthed in my spirit. But God was preparing an experience that would forever be etched in my mind and define the heart of my ministry.

During one particular training session, all the pace groups had completed the course together, as was the "impact" custom. But it quickly became evident that one of the runners had not yet reached the finish. So as a unified group, we all turned back and re-ran the course we had just completed in search of our running mate.

As we proceeded down the path, Jason's words kept running through my thoughts, "Everyone needs someone to come back for them."

With that in mind, each time my feet hit the ground there seemed to be an increased understanding of the "impact" concept.

When the team rounded a bend, there she was walking alone.

Exhausted, head hung, and barely able to shuffle one foot in front of the other, she looked defeated.

Discouraged.

Then she saw us coming toward her.

I will never forget the look on her face. It was beautiful. The look of feeling abandoned and forsaken was immediately transformed into a look of relief and gratitude.

Her smile indicated that her value had been affirmed. She hadn't been forgotten. Her tear-filled eyes expressed her elation and thankfulness; someone had come back for her.

Suddenly I flashed back to the days when I had been that

girl, feeling alone and insignificant. And it was God, and the people He had strategically placed in my path, that had come back for me time and again.

That was the impact Jason had been describing. First, the moments that God refuses to forsake us, and then the moment He connects us to someone whose heart has been discouraged and whose life has experienced defeat.

That day I decided I would make it my life's mission to always go back for those who are forgotten and left alone on the path of life. I wanted to be a person who was willing to come back, and then re-walk the road in order to show God's restorative power and make an impact on hurting lives.

As is always the case with God, He leads us to moments of decision and commitment in preparation for increased opportunities. My increased opportunities were to be found on the campus of Oak Ridge Elementary School in the Oak Park neighborhood of Sacramento. Economically impoverished, the area was a hot spot for despair and brokenness. Some of the children who crossed my path had life stories that rivaled even mine. Now God had placed me in an after school program that would totally immerse me in the reality of their lives.But when He placed me there, He also promised that whatever I did for the kids, He would bring healing to my life as well.

For some, the opportunity would have been overwhelming. These were kids who came to school hungry, wearing hand-me down clothes, and shoes with holes. Most were disheveled and rough around the edges, their hopelessness often expressed through anger or an attitude of indifference.

Each day I was on campus and looked into their faces, I saw the person I had once been, and I wanted to be that smile, that hug, that kind word, that would allow them to see the possibilities that existed, in spite of their current plight.

Because of the church and state boundaries, the Be Change team was not allowed to share our faith in God with the students or parents. So the message of His love and concern had to be demonstrated in very practical and tangible ways. We started a Tuesday morning coffee session for parents to attend, allowing us to connect with them and encourage their involvement in the education process.

Often when the hungry students heard we had pastries and fruit for the meetings, they would congregate outside the door, asking if they could just have a little something to fill their empty stomachs.

I understood the need was great, and because the quantity of food we brought with us each time was limited, I had been cautioned with the reality — "we can't feed them all."

But for the kids who would continue to stand outside the door, unashamed to swallow their pride and express their need, I knew I had to respond in any way I could. So when staff wasn't looking, I would frequently stuff food into the kids' backpacks and tell them to go eat in the restroom so no one would see them.

There's no denying that in comparison to the need, my

deed was miniscule. But at least I knew that every Tuesday, six or seven students would know the love of God through an act of kindness. Much like I did as a waif of a kid, when an elderly woman shared her blue tin of shortbread cookies with me. Knowing the impact her kindness had made on my life, I prayed that my expressions would linger in the students' hearts as well.

The Be Change team also organized a project called "Special Deliveries," which allowed us to respond to the practical needs of the school families. Receiving donations from our church families, we were able to deliver refrigerators, furniture, and beds to needy households. There was an amazing outpouring of gratitude with each delivery—from the family who for months had stored their food and perishables in ice chests, to children receiving a bed for the first time in their lives. We also provided weekly bags of food, and delivered clothes and shoes to the families, all in an effort to demonstrate God's provision at the point of their need.

As time went on, I became a celebrity of sorts when I walked onto the playground. Kids would run to greet me, smiling as if they were welcoming their best friend. There were always plenty of hugs throughout the afternoon, them for me, and me for them.

There were moments of trying to listen and decipher ten excited conversions at once, with me being mindful to acknowledge and respond to each one.

There were moments of tears when children would

share the heaviness of their hearts, and also happy tears when I commended them for a job well done.

There were looks of pleasant surprise when I remembered a small detail of their lives, and a sense of honor when I shared a small detail of mine with them.

There were moments of laughter and silliness, and times I'd line up with the girls to jump rope or dance horribly to a popular song.

With each encounter, every action and gesture was made in hopes that not one would feel left behind.

The more time I spent with the kids, the less I focused on their hopelessness. God was directing me to focus instead on their restoration. I began speaking words of affirmation as often as I had the chance. I continually assured them of their value and worth, knowing full well that even if they couldn't accept it in that moment, the words would become a seed of hope that would not be forgotten and one day take root in their hearts.

I found the more I affirmed them and prayed for their restoration, the more real and alive my own restoration felt. The impact I was allowed to make in these broken lives had brought another layer of healing to my heart, allowing me to stand more firmly and confidently in His plan for me.

As blessed as I had been to express my calling in the school arena, God was already preparing future opportunities that would have more far-reaching effects.

One of the families I became connected with at the school included four young girls who were being raised by their mom, aunt, and grandmother. I met the girls when they were in the third and fourth grades, and am honored to report I am still connected with them today.

I call them "my girls."

Because I responded to God's challenge of faithfulness in the lives of the underserved, He was able to accomplish more than I could ask or think in that environment. He developed and established a friendship with the girls beyond the school borders, allowing me to share my faith and story of God's faithfulness.

Over the years the girls attended summer youth camp and came to faith in Christ. They currently serve within the church, and are finishing high school and attending college. God has prepared their lives to impact those around them, further expanding His plan to restore and redeem wounded hearts.

Through my involvement in the internship program, more people at church were becoming aware of the story that had been my life. I was often approached by people who could not believe a person with such a strong presence in the church had ever experienced such hardship.

While I considered their comments a testament to God's grace and mercy in my life, I began to wonder if their surprise represented a failure on my part to be forthcoming with my testimony. Even though I wanted to use my experiences to help people, and was agreeable to answer questions any time they came up, I had to ask myself if I had been willing to share my story openly. And if I hadn't, why not?

My Girls!

It was then God began to challenge me about transparency, and that was a very uncomfortable proposition. Up to that point, I had been truly transparent with only a select few, mainly because a person with my past was not usually the type you would find in ministry. I knew the broken people I ministered to would be receptive, but was concerned if the good people of the church knew where I'd come from, they might be less impressed with the person who was serving alongside them.

Throughout the healing process, Jason and Lynette, as well as two trusted friends had been very protective of me, wisely allowing me to mend my heart in privacy and confidentiality. But God was preparing me for openness on a much larger scale.

He was asking for the door that had been slightly ajar to be swung wide open so He could fully impact those who would intersect my path. Not surprisingly, standing on the threshold of that decision stirred a great deal of apprehension inside of me. Despite all of the positives in my life, I found myself extremely emotional about the prospect of transparency and exposure.

I cried often.

I would be in the church office and my puffy, red eyes would draw the question, "What's wrong?"

To which I would firmly insist, "I'm okay."

But I wasn't.

My desire to stay hidden and God's request to step forward were now a persistent battle inside me.

Sometimes I think the tears I didn't cry growing up were specifically saved and released in that phase of my healing. It was the culmination of all the hurt I experienced as a child colliding with the undeniable purpose God had planned for me as an adult. It was intense and painful, and I knew it was God's call to decision.

That moment of decision was confirmed one day when Jason spoke six powerful and challenging words, "It's not a time to cry."

He was right.

It was a time to overcome my fear and be in total pursuit of His plan and my purpose.

With those words I determined to set aside my

hesitation and address the theme of transparency that had become a consistent topic between God and myself. The more I considered His request, the more apparent it became that I was battling an old and powerful enemy.

I had fallen back into a façade in order to keep myself presentable and safe. Once I identified the adversary, I knew in order to break the stronghold that had emerged, I would have to face two former challengers: surrender and vulnerability.

My acceptance of both was relatively easy this time. I knew from past experience that God had only required from me those things that would move me forward. He had not once failed me or deserted me in a moment of change and growth. He had never doubled-back because He'd led me in a wrong direction, and never decided mid-way through that He had made a mistake in calling me.

As uncomfortable as the prospect of transparency seemed, I was convinced deep in my heart that it was meant to be an integral part of my journey toward complete restoration and effective ministry.

So looking the requirement of transparency square in the eye, I determined to trust God in His continued wisdom for my life. As I experienced numerous times before, my acceptance of His leading was the key to incredible opportunities I would never have imagined or expected.

Finally willing to share my story as a whole, I understood it was what God had prepared me for, and what He intended to use for His restoration in the lives of others.

My first speaking opportunity came on an Easter Sunday

at my church, Capital Christian Center. The senior pastor and Jason had come to me weeks earlier with a request that I share my story and testimony of restoration with thousands of people in three services. I was terrified, unsure if I was ready to be that exposed.

But, I had to trust that if God had put it on their hearts to ask, He had also planned and purposed the opportunity to reach wounded hearts.

I remember climbing the steps to the platform that morning, not sure if my legs would carry me to the pulpit where the pastor was standing.

I was shaking.

My heart was pounding.

I had never been so nervous.

At the same time, as I began to speak, I had never felt so at peace. Because in that moment, I knew I was standing in the center of God's will for my life. All the life-notes that had once sounded so disconnected and unappealing, were melded together to reveal a beautiful symphony in His honor.

Soon I began receiving speaking opportunities in juvenile detention centers, prisons, schools, and women's groups. In each venue, response to the message and transparency was moving, as I watched God break down barriers and begin a healing work in broken lives. It was then I made a promise to God, to honestly and openly be His hand extended, knowing with certainty that He would use it for His glory.

In 2008, a full time position opened at the church, and

I was hired to work with our "Champions" ministry, which served the congregation's special needs children and adolescents. I also continued to assist Jason with our outreach ministries, which included organizing food and lodging programs for the homeless community, and coordinating back-to-school barbeques and family dinners for the school we partnered with through Be Change.

In both of these areas, it was important to me that we made an impact, ensuring no one felt left behind or insignificant. Near the holidays, we wanted the homeless to know they were not forgotten as we distributed food, clothes, and toiletries.

For the inner-city kids going back to school, we wanted to wish them a good year with a family barbeque and backpacks and needed supplies. And for those with special needs, often overlooked and forgotten, we wanted them to be observed and treated as the royal children of God they were.

While it was fairly easy to organize and execute events for the homeless and disadvantaged school programs, it became increasingly clear that the special needs community was severely underserved. Not just within our church walls, but in the community as a whole. Eager to reach out to the special needs community in a tangible way, and to bring inclusion to teens and young adults with disabilities, I presented our pastoral staff with my vision for "Evening of Dreams"— a prom-like event for individuals so often excluded from activities that are normal for many others their age.

With full approval from leadership, we began planning for our first Evening of Dreams event, set to debut in May 2009. We decided our prom would be a first-class, red carpet event, with our special needs guests being personally escorted by formally-dressed area athletes and student leaders. The evening would be complete with pre-prom hair styling and make-up, limousine arrivals, photographers, elaborate decorations, dinner, and an evening of entertainment and dancing.

As expected, there were some congregants who were opposed to the plan, but I believed God had birthed the idea in my heart as an opportunity to demonstrate His love in a unique and powerful way. I also believed if God was in our efforts, He would bless the event in an undeniable, undisputable manner. And the evidence of His approval far exceeded our wildest expectations, with every person involved in the event receiving a blessing beyond compare.

When we went to the local high schools proposing the idea to athletes and student leaders, we were overwhelmed by the number of young men and women who immediately volunteered to be escorts. The majority of students had never been exposed to individuals with special needs, but in spite of the unknown, were moved with compassion by the opportunity to make an impact.

Athletes who wore their names on their backs, for whom people cheered, and every day was their day, were willing to be anonymous for the sake of giving someone else the spotlight and making their dream come true.

We considered that God's first stamp of approval on the

event: the character and hearts of our volunteers would be profoundly impacted, and they could use their experiences to bring back awareness and influence to their campuses and peers.

We found the same overwhelming response within the business community, with eateries and retail establishments in the Sacramento area donating food, beverages, and keepsakes for the guests.

Even the local fire department participated in the festivities, granting one guest's dream to walk the red carpet with a fireman in full gear.

Congregants of the church also flooded bleachers that lined the entrance of the venue, clapping and cheering as each guest arrived and took that magical walk on red. There were many moments, with many arrivals, that it would have been hard to find a dry eye. God's second stamp of approval: hearts understanding that even in the smallest action, we can be God's hand extended.

The Evening of Dreams event delighted our special needs guests. The guests arrived ready to party — refusing to accept limitations of any kind.

The normally shy, invisible teen was suddenly transformed into a celebrity on stage. The guests who smiled from ear to ear were the same teens who had been trapped in their isolation. It was an amazing and beautiful display of the incredible value God places on every person, regardless of the packaging.

God's final stamp of approval on the event was seen in the parents and family members. For many of these individuals, they'd always been told their child was "different", and they carried that burden of exclusion on their behalf.

With Evening of Dreams we wanted the families to be able to connect with their children in a new way, witnessing joyful expressions and confidence they'd never seen before. For the moms and dads, brothers and sisters, grandmas and grandpas, we wanted it to be a God encounter; for them to know what it was like for Heaven and earth to collide. The event did just that. As we watched, families weep as they witnessed God's love showered without reservation on their child.

Evening of Dreams continues to be an annual event, bringing awareness and a tangible expression of God's love to the special needs community. (www.eveningofdreams.com)

After we concluded our first Evening of Dreams event, I returned home late that night and plopped into bed with all of my excitement and exhaustion. As I recalled all the memorable moments of the day, and offered gratitude to God for His help and guidance in the preparations and execution of the event, I became aware that He had once again used His plans to bring healing and restoration to my heart.

To fulfill the vision for the evening, I had worked tirelessly to ensure our guests understood their significance, and witnessed them flourishing in that truth. As I considered that determination and effort, I realized God

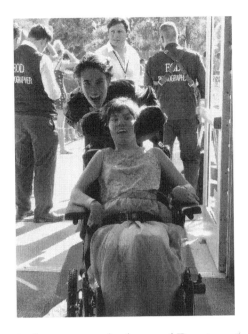

A glimpse into the heart of Evening of
Dreams.

had demonstrated very clearly that it was because of my own significance, through the value He unconditionally placed on me, that I was able to express my purpose and flourish in my calling.

In that moment of realization, I felt just as loved and important as any guest that we had ministered to that night.

As I continued to serve in the areas of ministry to which God had called me, I was determined to follow His guidance and direction for my life, confident that in doing so, He would be faithful to reveal the best version of me. On every occasion that I was given the opportunity, I went back for the forgotten and spoke words of affirmation and life to the underserved and disenfranchised.

I also continued the Evening of Dreams vision, determined that each subsequent year rivaled the one before, and ensuring that dreams and wishes continued to come true.

It was in this season of time that God began to stir my heart for completeness in my own life. While it had taken a backseat to the opportunities of ministry over the past years, I, too, desired dreams come true and the happy ending.

Although I wasn't exactly sure what that meant or should look like, I was determined to let God fill in the blanks with the perfect elements for complete and total restoration.

14

With an Open Heart: Promises and Possibilities

By 2010, God had blessed me immeasurably. Ministry opportunities were continually presenting themselves, and new and deeper friendships were developing. Under the watchful and loving care of Jason and Lynette over the previous three years, I had grown stronger and more confident, both emotionally and spiritually. In a sense, the environment God provided for me had been an incubator, warming me as I developed and keeping me safe until it was time to hatch and begin a new life that was healthy and secure.

In an emotional sense, God used those three years to give me a crash course on family life as it should be, and because the experience was meant both for healing and preparation, I was allowed to view the process from multiple viewpoints.

The insecure child in me had learned about the nurturing and protective nature of parents, as love was expressed and expectations and lessons of accountability were shared. Observing each family member's role on a daily basis I learned about obligation to one another in showing respect, support, and loyalty. And as the adult, sometimes being asked by Jason to step into a role of responsibility for the children's safety and well-being, I learned that dependability and trustworthiness matter immensely to the impressionable ones in our care.

In a spiritual sense, God used the three years at Jason's as an accelerated classroom. Just as He was narrowing the emotional gap between the wounded child and the rescued woman, He was constantly revealing Himself as wise in His leading, and faithful to supply His strength in my weakness. He had transformed me from a woman who imagined a purpose to one who was living and fulfilling her purpose.

Though the process had been challenging, and at times His instruction didn't make sense for the moment I was in, He continued to faithfully prepare me for each new ministry opportunity He intended to send my way.

That is perhaps one of the most amazing truths about God: given the opportunity, He will restore completely so that we may walk in absolute wholeness and abundance.

Throughout the incubation period, it wasn't enough to simply heal the spirit of a broken child — He wanted to mature the child so that she and the woman of promise could walk hand in hand into life's purpose. The restoration was not just for that moment. It wasn't an item on God's to do list, that once finished He could check off and move on to another project.

The restoration was also meant for preparation.

He had allowed me to experience emotional healing and participate in a thriving, loving family so that I would be capably prepared to manage and nurture the home and family He envisioned for me. He also purposed that the demonstration of His grace and mercy through each growth experience, was meant to effectively equip me with compassion and understanding for the ministry doors He intended to open.

May I pause here to declare once again, that God's mercy — His unmerited favor toward us, and His grace — His willingness to understand and forgive, is simply amazing.

It doesn't matter how many pieces a life has collapsed into, or how long we have held those pieces, He is faithful to mend and restore. As we give our unreserved permission, He will lovingly fulfill His promise to bring beauty from ashes, and I will never cease to celebrate that truth.

Recognizing the strength I had gained in my heart and spirit, I decided to step out and pursue life beyond my comfort zone, which meant leaving Jason's home and living in a different environment. While it was hard to leave the family and the security I had enjoyed for three years, I realized that change was necessary if I wanted to discover new facets of my life and faith. Much like staying on the same bus, the route you travel will never be anything more than what it has been. It requires a change in bus in order for the journey and experiences to be fresh and inspiring.

After leaving Jason's, I became roommates with a woman I met at the church. It was a great environment, with plenty of support and camaraderie. But as comfortable and happy as I felt, there was a stirring in my heart for a place I could call home, someplace that was mine, allowing me to plant roots and start a family. The desire had become a repetitive theme in my mind, but having dated very little since my arrival in Sacramento, I was obviously facing a significant deficit.

Hopeful, but not desperate, I continued to immerse myself in my church duties, praying for God's direction in every detail of my life.

In January 2011, I received an unexpected Facebook message. Joe, the man I had met in college, contacted me after I posted a picture of myself on a mission trip in Brazil. I had always liked Joe's personality and enjoyed our interactions. We had been Facebook friends since 2006, so occasionally corresponded, but nothing specific or terribly personal. But after a few messages back and forth about my experiences in the ministry, Joe asked if it would be possible to talk and catch up.

Wait. What? You're married, dude! was my immediate thought.

But continuing to read, Joe shared that much had happened over the years, including an unanticipated divorce, and a renewed consecration to God's authority and direction in his life. I was intrigued, and anxious to understand why, out of all the women he had met in his travels, I was the one with whom he was trying to reconnect. It was a touching story, and perhaps one best told by Joe himself:

"I self-admittedly have an aversion to social media. Just ask Michelle and she'll confirm this. I don't think it's all bad; I just have a hard time totally wrapping my brain around the whole thing. If it weren't for the Facebook community that Mark Zuckerburg created, I wouldn't be able to share my part of this amazing journey you've taken the time to read about over the past several chapters.

Michelle and I first met at college in Edwardsville, IL in 2000.

I had no idea at the time that this cute, funny, bubbly girl had been through the tempest of an upbringing that she had endured. I also had no idea that this same girl, that lived two doors down from me and was a teammate of mine on the track and field team, would someday become my beautiful wife and the amazing mother of our two children.

I wish I could say that there was instant chemistry when we met all those years ago, but unfortunately, I can't. Over the course of college we were just friends. Although I did have a flash in the pan crush on her for a small time, it was never something I pursued (or even told her about). Honestly, at that time in my life, I wasn't the man that I should have been.

Over the next ten years, my baggage went from carried on and stored in the overhead bin to checking multiple bags. So I believe that God was protecting and preparing both of us (heart, soul, and mind) for the journey we would someday take together.

His timing and plan is always better than ours. And He has already paid for all of our baggage fees.

Thankfully, we both made it through the college haze, for the most part unscathed. After this we moved onto what we thought was next in our lives. I tried my hand with a group of some of my closest friends and brothers to make an impact on the music world, and Michelle was moving into her career as well.

We really didn't keep in touch for several years. Around 2006, we became friends on MySpace and later Facebook. Over the years we stayed in touch with an email or check-in every so often, mostly to say I hope things are going well for you. As I said earlier, I have an aversion to social media, but what I didn't realize at that time is that it actually helped water the seeds that I didn't even know God was planting in my heart for the woman that would someday stand next to me as my bride.

After the dreams that I had of becoming a music superstar faded with the spotlight, I felt God directing me back to my passion for learning. Without telling anyone, I began to search out graduate school programs. This led me to the next six and a half years of my life, which I spent between Murray and Lexington, Kentucky. This period was both a time of tremendous personal growth and a time of testing. I've heard it said that strength is never gained unless you're faced with resistance. I definitely learned this the hard way, but am grateful that God's grace is stronger than our greatest weakness.

I've never felt such a God-sized bear hug as what I did following my time in Kentucky.

So how did an Illinois born-and-bred guy living in the Bluegrass state end up marrying a California transplant who grew up less than 50 miles from my hometown? If you ask Michelle to tell this part of the story, she will tell you that I was stalking her on Facebook (she's entitled to her opinion).

In all honesty, I really don't know. After seeing a picture she had posted, I commented that she looked beautiful. Looking back now I think that it was God's way of slapping me upside the head and telling me to buckle up. After all, because she was living in Sacramento and I was living in Lexington, 2,300 miles separated us.

In January of 2011, we reconnected and the first phone conversation lasted more than three hours! It was spent catching up, laughing, and talking about how life had taken us on very different paths. Over the next few months, we kept in touch and talked more often. During many late nights, and even one all night phone call, we grew increasingly close. It wasn't until my cousin asked me if there was something going on between us that we really talked about what both of us were feeling, but both had been dancing around. If you ask Michelle, dancing is not one of my strong suits. But that's alright, I still got the girl.

After joking about meeting for a sushi date halfway in between Sacramento and Lexington (we actually looked up the spot), we decided to get together in St. Louis for our first official date when Michelle was in town for a friend's wedding. This would be the first time we had seen each other in person in almost ten years. I was so nervous that I stepped on her foot when we saw each other.

Casanova and Fred Astaire would not have been proud.

*Luckily the rest of the day went better. We did it all —
breakfast, card games, sushi, and a St. Louis Cardinals game, all
in one day. I kept asking myself, "Am I really falling for this girl?"*

*After our St. Louis adventure, we still weren't certain of our
future. We decided to pray about it and see where God led us.
Michelle hopped an early flight back to Sacramento the next
morning, and I'm pretty sure I sang old Bon Jovi tunes all the
way back to Lexington, with a smile on my face wider than the
Gateway Arch.*

*It wasn't until after Michelle's visit to Kentucky in August of
that year we knew that God had truly brought us together. We
knew we wanted to spend the rest of our lives together.*

*So in October of 2011, I put "Going to California" by Led
Zepplin on repeat in my headphones and boarded a plane to see
Michelle and ask a question that would be the next step, as God
was getting ready to add the two colors of paint that had been our
lives separately into one beautiful masterpiece that only He can
take the credit for painting.*

*After spending a Friday in San Francisco, and on the next to
last day of the trip, we decided to have a relaxing day together.
After lunch and a day on the town, we went back to the house to
relax and watch a movie. After the movie was over, Michelle went
to freshen up and I sat in the living room to "read".*

*Michelle hollered from the back, asking if I had taken her Bible
from her room. I'm about as good a thief as I am a dancer. When
she came into the living room I asked her to sit beside me on the
fireplace. I told her that I wanted to share a few things that I had
been reading a lot lately that had been stirring my heart. I read*

a passage in Ephesians 5, and a few things I had been journaling about.

I also read a mission statement that I had written about the type of husband I wanted to be for her.

Tears began to flow down both our faces (they are flowing down mine again as I'm typing this). I was staring at the woman that I was going to spend the rest of my life with — the woman that I was going to start and raise a family with. The woman I was going to share my heart and soul with.

Since you've read this far in the book, you know that Michelle had several different last names growing up and struggled heavily with her identity and not knowing her real last name.

I told her that one thing I felt God wanted me to give her was the gift of a last name, and to be a part of a family and heritage founded on faith and love. He wanted her to be able to pass that along to our future children as their inheritance. And even though I couldn't do that immediately, I could give her the first step toward that.

Then on October 29, 2011, I asked her to marry me."

As Joe shared, from January through May, we communicated daily, sharing our deepest thoughts and desires for God's blessing in our lives. I shared much about my past, concerned at first that the woman he had been intrigued with on Facebook, would be less desirable when seen in a new light. But the truth of my past and brokenness did nothing to intimidate or deter him, so I began to wonder if this was the man God had selected and prepared to be my life-mate and partner.

In June 2011 we met in St. Louis, and then in August of that year I traveled to Illinois to meet Joe's family. I immediately fell in love with his parents, their acceptance and approval of me was something I'd never experienced before. It was overwhelming and terrifying and wonderful all at the same time.

The more time I spent with them on subsequent visits, the more I knew I wanted to join this kind and generous Christian family, and raise my children surrounded by this kind of love.

Interestingly, before I met Joe's family, his mother had a dream about him. She dreamt their family was in a large church she didn't recognize, but it was apparent they were at Joe's wedding and a blonde girl was standing next to him. After meeting and getting acquainted with me, she shared the dream with Joe and confidently confided, "That's my new daughter."

October 2011 found Joe on bended knee, asking me to be his wife and share a future together. To be honest, the possibility found my heart and mind in a bit of a tug-of-war, wondering if I was worthy enough of the blessing. It was something I wanted, for sure, but in the back of my mind I had continued to equate the degree of God's blessings with my worth. Quite a contrast from the heart of my ministry, where I believed in the incredible value of the kids I worked with, and knew God wanted to bless them with success and happiness.

At the time it seemed a bit easier to believe that for others than it did for myself. But having been in prayer about the relationship for months, and receiving wise counsel regarding the Father's desire to bless my life, I accepted Joe's proposal. So in April 2012, Joe moved to Sacramento, established his new career, and we began planning for a July wedding.

There were just a few months to prepare for the festivities, and while most brides-to-be might have been stressed by the time constraints, the day couldn't come soon enough for me. It was a dream come true to plan every detail, and just as my life had been beyond the norm, I was determined my wedding day would be the same. Tradition would certainly play a significant role, but I also wanted the occasion to reflect me and the meaningful elements that had shaped my life over the past years in Sacramento.

It was July 20, 2012 at 6:00 p.m. The auditorium of our church, Capital Christian Center, was simply yet elegantly decorated. The four stairs leading to the platform, as well as the four-tier choir stage at the back of the platform, were lined with candles of all different shapes and sizes. The golden glow made the spot where Joe and I would exchange our vows inviting and warm. Behind the choir stage there were three white linen cloths draped from ceiling to floor. Piano music was playing in the background, setting a magical tone for the evening.

My sixteen bridesmaids, each dressed in white, one with pink hair, some with tattoos, walked in pairs to meet their escorts, then stood in a staggered pattern on the platform steps. My two flower girls also dressed in white, adorably scattered petals down the long aisle of the 3,000-seat auditorium.

But the most precious part of the pre-ceremony moments was the entrance of 14 of the children from Oak Ridge Elementary School, the students with whom I had connected over the past years.

I watched with pride as they lined up to make their entrance into the auditorium, each one of them honored by their role and reverencing the moment just for me. They wore white button-down shirts and carried candles, positioning themselves down the center aisle. For some it was the first time they'd ever dressed up, and the only time others had ever been inside a church.

It was a beautiful sight.

Moments before my entrance, Jason stepped to the center of the platform and informed the guests of my preferred reception. I wanted everyone to remain seated, so as I passed each row, I could look at the faces of those who had so lovingly supported me. From the students to my church family, from the Rands who sat on the front pew as my surrogate parents to my future family, I wanted to honor each person who had expressed God's love and goodness to me throughout the many phases of my life.

As the auditorium's double doors opened, revealing my dream-come-true, our senior pastor, Rick Cole, linked his arm through mine and smiled like a proud father would have.

As we walked slowly down the aisle, I took special note of the faces, smiles, and tears that approved and celebrated each step. Then I looked forward, and there was Joe standing in a gray suit, smiling from ear-to-ear. It was all I could do at that point not to forsake the bride's traditional saunter and run to meet the love of my life.

When our final step brought the pastor and I to the front of the church, a song began. I remember the lyrics perfectly matched my and Joe's desire for life together: "Guide us with your grace, give us faith so we'll be safe."

I looked at Joe, he was wiping tears from his eyes, which brought tears to mine. Midway through the song the lyrics faded and Jason stepped again to center stage. He smiled at me, confirming he knew exactly how long the road had been, and how awesomely God had blessed. Then, as if acknowledging all my determination and hard work, he beamed and said, "This is your moment."

With those words, chills of thankfulness and gratitude covered me. Jason continued by asking, "Who gives Michelle to be married to Joe?"

Pastor Rick responded, "Cathy and I do on behalf of our Capital Christian Center family."

With that Joe stepped toward me and took my arm.

It was the safest I had ever felt, knowing that God had given me this wonderful man for life. Totally engrossed in the moment, I broke pre-vow etiquette and snuck a little kiss as the song resumed and concluded.

By that time Pastor Rick had moved to the center of the platform to officiate over the ceremony. He began by speaking directly to me, "Michelle, you have a gift of making people feel connected to you." With that statement I thought specifically of the Oak Ridge kids who had lined the aisle in my honor. My past had allowed me to identify with their struggles and challenges, and our connection had brought them to this moment.

The candles the kids carried were very symbolic to me. They represented the broken life I had once led. Then when cued, the kids blew out the candles in unison, symbolizing that I was leaving my past behind. As I stood there, the recipient of God's amazing grace, I felt as if I represented hope for all their lives as well. I knew firsthand the possibilities God planned for each of them, and that truth thrilled my heart almost as much as the moment itself.

Pastor Rick continued by advising Joe and I that we were a gift, each one to the other. Then we stepped onto the platform to light the unity candle, signifying our desire and commitment to join our hearts and lives together. Once the unity candle was lit, a video was shown depicting our journey from friendship to marriage. A friend had taken us both to a beautiful vineyard, and filmed us separately sharing our hearts about the other. It was then edited to create a beautiful story that we would both see for the first time at the wedding. The alternating video clips went like this:

I described my excitement to be married and have someone to come home to. For years I had watched couples share love and secrets, stories and memories. And now, I too would experience the joy of having someone special with whom I could share.

Joe spoke about his excitement to marry his best friend and to have a family to whom we would pass on an inheritance of unconditional love. Then sheepishly he said, "And I'm looking forward to the honeymoon, too."

The auditorium erupted with laughter. To which Joe responded with a smile and a wink to the guests behind us.

I explained that I met Joe in college eleven years prior, and that I was "pretty sure he was stalking me". Our guests laughed. Then I recounted how we had parted ways and unexpectedly reconnected, and that I was so thankful.

Joe shared that before me, he felt like he was stuck and wasn't moving forward. When we reconnected, he wasn't really looking for anything more than catching up with an old friend, he said. But once we got reacquainted, he was anxious to see how things would develop, which gave him something wonderful to look forward to.

The clip that followed was of me, sharing a bit more of my heart and story. I stated that growing up, I didn't know who my real dad was, and that I was moved from home to home, each time taking the last name of the family I lived with. I expressed my difficulty with never having a clear identity, and how that sets the stage for not knowing who you are or who you're meant to be.

In the next clip, Joe shared that since reconnecting and spending time with me, he had been journaling and searching God's word for His plan for our relationship. Then Joe teared up, and expressed that through his soul searching, he knew he wanted to give me the gift of a last name, so that I would know I had a family, and know who I was.

I don't believe there was one dry-eyed guest in the

auditorium. I cried too, because not only had I found my Prince Charming, but he was professing his desire and intent to fulfill my life-long yearning to belong and have a name of my own.

After the video, the ceremony continued with Joe and I sharing a beautiful communion officiated by Joe's father. Then with the exchanging of vows and rings, and a blessing over our future, we were pronounced husband and wife.

As I mentioned earlier in this chapter, my wedding was meant to reflect me, as evidenced by the victory dance I broke into upon the proclamation of marriage. When the pastor instructed Joe to kiss his bride, I motioned for my man to *come and get it*. There was laughter and applause, and it was the most wonderful compliment to the most beautiful day of my life.

And after the introduction of Mr. and Mrs. Joe Raby, my new husband and I gleefully exited the auditorium to the song *"Signed, Sealed, Delivered"* by Stevie Wonder.

The reception was magical. The tables were decorated with candles, and a dessert buffet was elegantly prepared. For part of the evening, Joe and I were found in the center of the room dancing with the Oak Ridge children. We had an amazing time. The joy on the children's faces was one of the best gifts of the evening. Several times after Joe left us to go visit with guests, I would attempt to break away, telling the kids I needed to spend some time with my husband, too.

When I would look around to spot him, I would find Joe watching the children and me smiling from ear to ear. It was

Mr. and Mrs.

in those moments I realized God had outdone Himself for me once again.

He had given me a man who fully understood how important ministry would be in my life, and he was willing and prepared to whole-heartedly support me in my calling.

Following a wonderful honeymoon, Joe and I settled into daily life, with God constantly affirming His blessing on our union. Looking at life through the eyes of a partnership was a completely new experience for me.

For so long I had been self-reliant, and now God had gifted me with an amazing support system. No longer would I have to dream alone, or shoulder challenges, or experience triumphs on my own. Instead, God had given me a partner who would bring balance and harmony to a life-story that had started out quite differently.

With God's heart melded with Joe's, it was as if the King Himself had sent the prince to deeply love the girl who had experienced such hardship and distress. And there was no one who could have supported and loved me more unconditionally, more completely, than God and Joe.

I remember the first time I truly understood that truth, and recognized the incredible significance of my partnership with Joe, and ours with God. I had a speaking engagement at a church. Joe sat on the first row recording my talk with his phone. In the same audience was a woman who snapped a picture of Joe, enthralled as he watched me speak about God's amazing grace in my life. The picture she captured was moving. Joe was holding the phone in one hand, and with his other hand was covering his mouth as if to conceal a quivering lip. The picture didn't zoom in on Joe's face, but if it had, I believe it would have captured tears of empathy and admiration and pride for me.

The picture overwhelmed me — I understood that God had brought me full circle. I had given my story to Him, and not only was He allowing me to share it to impact the lives of others, He was also allowing me to see the evidence of His restoration sitting on the front row.

In that instant I knew that every challenge I had faced in life, every time I had veered off course, God was behind the scenes orchestrating the very moment His plan and purpose would establish victory over the hardships meant to defeat me.

In Joe's care over the months that followed, my heart began to open to all the value God had placed in me. The unconditional support and constant words of affirmation were instrumental in developing my strength and confidence, allowing me to approach new opportunities with assurance and enthusiasm. The deep desire to write my life story perhaps the most telling of the continued healing that was occurring in my heart each day. While years ago I may have assumed that the restoration of hearts has a beginning and an end, I now believe that moments of healing and growth are meant to be ongoing, allowing us daily to see God in new and incredible ways.

In 2012, Joe and I learned we were going to be parents, and immediately we began to discuss the mission and vision for our home. We determined that our family foundation would be built on security and stability, and that our first priority would be to always speak words of life to each other as well as to our children. We were determined that with God, His principles, guidance, and approval, we would ensure a future of promise for our family.

Once again I recognized the significance of my past to my present. Of all the places my life could have journeyed to, His grace and mercy had brought me to this moment, allowing me to create a future of promise from a redeemed past. And the solid foundation my family would enjoy, despite the rockiness of my own, was one of the most amazing gifts I could have ever imagined.

Proof once again that God, when given an opportunity

and our permission, will exceed our expectations and transcend the realm of probabilities for divine possibilities.

ooo

Despite all the miracles God had performed in my life, and the blessings I was experiencing every day, deep in my subconscious there was still a hesitancy to believe that my past wouldn't somehow tarnish my present. So when my blessings met the ultimate challenge, the threads woven into my early life's tapestry created the backdrop for the all the panic that surfaced in the hospital the day of Cohen's delivery.

For me, it became a pivotal moment of decision that offered only two choices: I could continue to allow the past to intimidate the girl God had rescued and redefined, or I could totally commit to His redemption for my life.

In my fear and apprehension, I knew that God's faithfulness in my life was far more powerful than the traces of my past. And no matter the conclusion, whether joy or pain, I knew God would be trustworthy in all His ways.

15

With God: Miracles

The nurse's words, "Eleven minutes", kept ringing in my ears as the rush of activity continued in the corner. My mind acknowledged God was in control. I knew He was in the center of the critical moments that were ticking away. I knew with one Divine breath He could give life to my son. I knew it! Yet my anguished heart made one last fearful expression, "But he's not okay."

And in the very moment my fear was expressed, God, in His loving kindness, graciously whispered into my heart, "Oh, but he is."

With God's assurance expressed, and a decision to completely trust, I said to Joe, "We need to pray."

As we bowed our heads, and as our friends in the room prayed, I placed my son into the hands of the God who had always outdone Himself on my behalf, the God who was stronger than my fears, and who had redeemed my past for an amazing future.

As we prayed, our hearts leapt with hope as we heard Cohen's first weak cry. As quickly as our hopes were raised, they fell within moments as the nurse repeated, "He's not breathing."

The room was silent with the exception of the medical staff as they continued to coax, command, and encourage our son to breathe. Then we heard it. Another faint cry, and then another.

Quickly the nurse wrapped Cohen in a blanket. She walked him over to my bed, allowing Joe and I to bond with him for the briefest of moments. Then he was whisked away to the infant intensive care unit. As the doctor stood to leave he offered his opinion on the events that had transpired, and expressed his belief that Cohen would be okay.

We knew somehow that the next hour would be critical.

With great consideration the nurse routinely informed us of the measures that were being taken on Cohen's behalf, and continually encouraged us with her belief that he was going to be just fine. At one point we noticed she hadn't come back to update or assure us for quite some time.

The room grew quiet again, and Joe and I decided he should go to the infant care unit to find out what was going on.

He squeezed my hand as he turned to leave.

I watched as he opened the door and stopped dead in his tracks. I couldn't see through the doorway, but knew that Joe had stopped for a reason. It was the nurse. She was walking quickly toward him. Joe turned and walked toward me, his eyes filled with tears. And following immediately behind was the most wonderful expression of God's love to me, to us — our baby boy Cohen.

It was four o'clock in the morning when he was placed in my arms, and we would spend the next hours enjoying our little miracle. We took inventory, marveling at his little ears, and feet, and skin. Joe pulled the stuffed giraffe out of the overnight bag and presented it to Cohen, "from Mommy and Daddy.

Then we reconnected with Joe's parents so they would have the opportunity to celebrate the newest addition with us. And as each of us considered the events of the past hours, our hearts were filled with awe and gratitude for the love and grace our Heavenly Father had shown.

In Mommy's arms

Today, Cohen is happy and healthy and the apple of our eye. He is a spirited four year-old who loves to sing worship songs while playing his toy guitar, and enthusiastically dresses as the super hero he wants to be when he grows up.

Our lives have also been blessed with a beautiful daughter, Annalee. She was born on Valentine's Day 2015, and has been one of the most amazing expressions of God's love to us.

She is sweet and inquisitive, and has a smile that can melt your heart. And her beautiful blue eyes daily sparkle with confidence, assuring us that she is secure in her identity and significance.

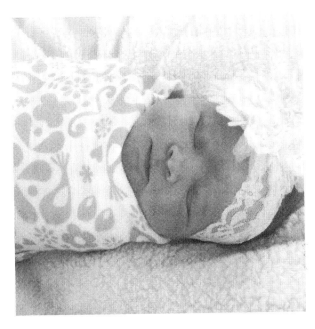

Our Sweet Annalee

As our family grows, we purpose to speak words of life every day, striving to instill in our children their value and worth, both to us and to God. In doing so, God has used those expressions to beautifully emphasize my own worth to Him, as well as my value to my family. There was no greater revelation of this truth, than during one family afternoon at the park.

As our family grows, we purpose to speak words of life every day, striving to instill in our children their value and worth, both to us and to God. In doing so, God has used those expressions to beautifully emphasize my own worth to Him, as well as my value to my family. There was no greater revelation of this truth, than during one family afternoon at the park.

The monkey bars, five rungs from start to finish, had caught Cohen's eye and he expressed his desire to swing on them. But struggling with the need to reach and swing his body at the same time, he dropped after only two rungs. Disappointed and ready to leave the challenge behind for something more manageable, we commented on how brave he was and how proud we were that he tried. And still seeing the desire in his eyes to swing on the bars, we excitedly encouraged him to try one more time.

This time I used my phone to record his attempt. With Annalee playing happily in the sand below, Cohen stood on the crossbar in his striped shirt. With Joe close at hand, he jumped from the crossbar to grab the first yellow rung, then the second. I was excitedly coaching him, "Show me what you got. Go to the next one. Good, good, good!"

He reached out and grabbed the third rung. Joe had positioned himself a little closer, cheering him on, "Good job, buddy. Come on, come on."

Then Cohen stretched and grabbed the fourth rung, but with only one hand. He dangled and swayed for a few seconds, with Joe still cheering but preparing himself to cushion the drop. I giggled with anticipation and excitement, anxious for him to make it to the final rung. Then, with his determination displayed by his protruding tongue, Cohen reached out and grabbed the fifth rung, with me yelling, "You got it!" and Joe giving a celebratory shout.

With a big smile, and a great accomplishment under his belt, Cohen released the bar and dropped to the ground below.

It is in moments like those, when I am supporting and encouraging my family, that God speaks volumes to my heart. I am reminded of all the times He was in my corner and sent people into my life to encourage me on His behalf. Only a Father who loves deeply and completely would worry about such details. And He did. From an elderly lady with a blue tin of cookies to friends who faithfully supported my dreams, He orchestrated all those things to emphasize my worth.

I am also reminded that His healing and restoration has prepared me to influence those around me. He has taken a vessel that was once cracked and dull, and made it priceless by filling me with His mercy and grace. Only a Father who recognizes true value would devote such love and attention. As I think of those I minister to, as well as my own children, I understand He has entrusted wounded, broken, and now impressionable young hearts to me for safe keeping. And with that, He has underscored my significance as His hand extended.

Daily I am amazed at God's investment in my life's story. I am honored by His faithfulness, astounded by His protection, and grateful for His unfailing love. The peace He's imparted for each broken piece I've placed in His hands, is unmatched and unsurpassed. The story may have begun with a broken little girl, but today she is transformed into a treasure of the Almighty King.

For as long as I have breath I will proclaim, with God my past is redeemed, my future is established, and my life is filled with promise.

PART V

The Exclamation Point

"God is perfect in love. In His wisdom He always knows what is best,
and in His sovereignty He has the power to bring it about."

~ Jerry Bridges

16

Far From Finished

The previous chapter was meant to be the last chapter of my story. It feels complete — a full circle journey depicting God's grace over my life. I was blessed with a wonderful ending to a broken beginning, and that certainly was more than enough for me.

But that was not God's plan.

Instead His intent was to outdo Himself once again on my behalf. And this time, His mighty hand would add an exclamation point I could have never imagined.

In July 2015, I was scheduled to be in a friend's wedding. So Joe, the kids, and I drove to Illinois to attend the weekend festivities, and to spend several weeks with Joe's parents and brothers. In making the preparations I also called my grandparents to let them know of our plans and to arrange to spend some time with them.

I was excited about the trip, anxious for both families

to see the kids again. But several days after our initial conversation, my grandmother called with a request that made my heart stop. It was a straightforward, out of the blue question that blindsided me.

Would you be willing to see your mom?

I was silent. Dumbfounded. Did she actually just ask that? I hadn't seen my mom in ten years. I hadn't spoken to her in eight. My grandmother knew that, and she certainly knew why. I sat down on a chair, my heart pounding and stomach turning. I swallowed hard and tried to make some words come out of my mouth. But I couldn't. I just sat motionless in the middle of this surreal, unimaginable moment.

Cautiously she began to respond to my silence.

She explained that over the past months my mom had been in and out of the hospital several times due to drug overdoses. The last incident was the most frightening. She almost died.

She went on to explain that the experience served as a wake-up call for my mom, and that she had been clean and drug-free for more than a month. When my grandmother's words stopped on the other end, all I could do was shake my head in disbelief.

The only response I could muster was, *I don't know.*

I immediately called Joe. I needed him to help make sense of the request and the feelings it stirred in my heart, and over the next few days it became the primary topic of discussion in our home. I knew I had Joe's support no matter what decision I made. I was confident with God's help and

Joe's encouragement I could successfully stand face to face with my past. But I didn't know if I wanted to open a door that had been closed and sealed so many years ago.

There was so much more at stake now.

My wonderful life, my healing, my personal growth, everything that was important to me would be exposed to all that had wounded me. With the exception of my children. If I went down this path, I had already determined I would not allow my mom to meet my children.

After praying several days for guidance in making the decision, I decided to share my dilemma with a few of our staff pastors. As they gathered around and prayed for me I felt assured that God had an answer to this life-altering decision. In the days following their prayer I felt as if the answer to my grandmother's request would be no, I would not meet with my mom.

In my mind there seemed to be little reason to step backwards, having moved so far forward in my life. Certainly God wouldn't expect me to jeopardize all He'd accomplished.

At least that's what I hoped.

During our drive to Illinois my heart and mind battled with my decision. Finally the struggle became so overwhelming that I decided I would meet with her, just to get it over with. Just to be done with the wondering and apprehension. With that decision my mind began the task of guarding my heart and preparing for the unknown. The process was reminiscent of my survival skills as a child.

With a call made to my grandmother, the time and place

was set for the meeting. I told Joe I would go alone, but the idea was quickly shot down. Joe expressed his intent to be present and supportive, and a protector, if needed. The reunion was scheduled for the Monday following the wedding, which was ideal, because at least for the weekend I could keep my mind occupied with uplifting things rather than playing out a thousand different scenarios in my head.

That Sunday afternoon Joe and I visited family friends who had played a significant role in our lives over the years. During the course of our conversation I revealed my intent to meet with my mom the following day. Because our friends were all too familiar with my background and struggles, there was an immediate silence in the room, an undeniable sense of disbelief.

I searched their faces, hoping for some wise counsel, or maybe some assurance I was making a good decision. Instead, my revelation was met with the understandable curiosity, *why would you do that?*

It was a good question.

Why, when it would have been so easy to say no, had I said yes? The choice to meet with my mom was the easy part. It was a generic, matter-of-fact decision. Either I would or wouldn't. But I hadn't given any thought to the motivation for the response. Now I was being confronted with the *why* of the decision, and I had to honestly examine my heart to understand the reason.

I looked at Joe. My face felt hot. I wasn't prepared to look so deep or be so vulnerable, but I also wasn't one to shy away from the tough questions once they were asked. I hesitated for a moment, knowing deep in my spirit that this was an opportunity to be real with myself and God. Then in an instant my entire life cycled through my mind. The bad and good, the failures and triumphs, the painful wounds and amazing healing. It was as if God brought my past and my present into focus, both intersecting and demanding a choice at the deepest level.

As I responded to the question I was taken aback by what my heart began to reveal. Openly I expressed that there had been so much bitterness and anger over the years — that I knew I couldn't be completely whole until there was forgiveness.

Over recent months I recognized that when I shared my story at speaking engagements, it should feel different. God had done a miraculous work in my life, yet the story felt unfinished. And I knew it wouldn't be as beautiful as it was meant to be until the work was complete. So there it was, in one of the most honest moments of my life, I understood the *why*.

The next morning Joe and I drove to the M & M Courtyard Café in Salem. I was quiet on the ride, processing the significance of the moments ahead. As we neared East Main Street Joe took my hand and asked if I was okay. I nodded nervously. My heart was pounding. I closed my eyes and took a deep breath, exhaling slowly and loudly. Joe sweetly reiterated that I didn't have to go through with it, but I knew with all I had faced and conquered over the years, I could do this too.

I stared out the car window. It was a warm, sunny day.

The streets were lined with early 1900's two and three-story brick buildings with ornate architecture. The charm of the small town was noticeable, but it almost felt too small given the life-altering event about to take place. We parked the car and walked hand-in-hand toward the café. A gray-brick, two-story courthouse was on one corner and city hall on the other. It all felt so formal.

Would the meeting feel the same way? An exchange of pleasantries, carefully chosen words which would neither assume guilt nor express pain, and a polite nod of the head when the uncomfortable dialog was over. My mind raced almost as fast as my heart. I clinched Joe's hand even tighter, but still not tight enough.

We arrived at the café. It was quaint and small. It had a large store front window shaded by a green and white striped awning, and was bordered by a small law office on one side and a corner park on the other. The park had benches, a center fountain, and a mural painted on the side of the building. For a moment I allowed myself to get lost in the serenity of the setting, the first calmness I'd felt in hours. Then Joe's gentle voice redefined the moment with the all-important question, *are you ready?*

I laced my arm through his and laid my head on his shoulder. Joe had never insisted I take this step, but I knew he believed it was the best thing for me personally, and for my ministry in the future. And I knew he was proud of me for courageously facing the fear and apprehension.

I exhaled forcefully, as if to rid my stomach of the

butterflies. Then I turned to Joe, my eyes silently expressing my decision to move forward no matter the outcome.

As we stepped into the café, I hesitated for a moment as I glanced around the room. It was strange. I suddenly realized I had no idea if I would be able to pick my mom out of the crowd. The café was small, so naturally all eyes turned our way when we came into the building.

But no stare lingered.

No one looked at me as if they were reconciling years of absence and separation.

No one stood to motion me over to her table.

Everyone simply refocused on their meals and pleasant conversations, oblivious to the fact that this stranger's life was about to change.

The oversized entryway of the café was adorned with knick-knacks and collectibles, and Joe began to browse his way through the narrow aisles. There was a large rotating globe on a wooden stand in the center of the clutter that caught my eye. It was a profound reminder that my life with my husband and children was a world away from the life I once led in Illinois. Worlds away, actually.

With another guest entering the café, I quickly scooted to one side of the entryway, making sure I didn't block access to the dining area. I refocused my attention on the collectibles, but out of the corner of my eye could see the well-dressed woman walking with a determined gait. I scooted over a bit further, careful not to slow her down. But my adjustment did not seem to change her direction. My first thought was maybe she was hurrying to get to the collectibles area. Then out of the corner of my eye I watched the woman stop directly beside me. I turned slowly, fully ready to apologize for obstructing the path.

When we made eye contact, the woman just stared at me. I smiled uncomfortably then turned to catch Joe's attention. When he looked up and saw the woman standing next to me, his face froze for a moment. Then with a slight smile and a nod, he acknowledged that this was it, the moment we'd been waiting for.

I swallowed hard, slowly turning again to look into the woman's face. I honestly didn't recognize her. The hair, the smile, the clothes did not represent the person I once knew. But in searching her eyes I found a hint of something familiar. Then in a moment of disbelief, I cautiously asked, "Is that you?"

To which she nervously responded, "It's me, baby."

Suddenly I was numb. It was as if everything had shifted into slow motion, with the noise in the restaurant fading to the sound of my heartbeat. Joe reached my side and quickly slipped a supportive arm around me. And as this surreal moment played out, the only thing I could utter was, "Do you want coffee?"

Once we were seated the conversation was awkward. I expressed my surprise that I didn't recognize her, and she shared that she had recently cut her hair and lost weight. After that exchange we simply sat staring in silence for a few moments, with me wondering *where do we go with this conversation.*

Finally I asked how she was doing, and it was as if I had

opened a book. She began to share how in January she had smoked a synthetic drug laced with random stuff and nearly died. She explained she had passed out, and that my brother had busted a window in the trailer to get to her. CPR had saved her and given her a second chance, but the lure of the drug found her in the same predicament several more times after that incident. It was when the doctor adamantly warned her that she was sick and dying, and may have used up all her chances, that she recognized her death was impending. She explained she believed that was her wake-up call, and she had been clean and sober ever since.

As she continued to speak, she divulged details of my family history. I listened intently as I discovered answers to questions I had always wondered about, occurrences and events long cloaked in secrecy. She also shared about the death of her father; the grandfather I had never known. Finally, stories about the jobs she had done, including working as a lunch lady in a cafeteria, completed the picture of what life had become for her.

To anyone passing the glass storefront, the conversation on the other side would have appeared benign, uneventful. To outside eyes it looked like nothing more than three friends sharing an afternoon chat. But in those moments it was as if a jigsaw puzzle had been spread out in front of me, and someone was handing me the pieces and saying *this goes here*. Blank spots were being filled in and a more complete picture was beginning to unfold.

When the conversation lulled, I looked down at the hot chocolate cup I had been constantly turning. It was empty now. The indicator, perhaps, that no more time was needed, that everything meant to be said had been. I looked at Joe and smiled weakly. He smiled back.

It was obvious he sensed my discomfort with the silence, but he made no suggestion that we needed to go. And while rescue would have been nice, it was apparent when Joe gently placed his hand on mine that he believed the afternoon was purposed for more.

I turned my attention back to my mom and found her staring at me. It was if the awkwardness of the moment paled for her. Her focus instead on reconciling the girl she remembered with the woman she just met. Looking each other in the eye, I suddenly felt nervous, unsure of what to do or say next. I felt my heart pound and my hands begin to tremble. Then, in an awkwardly casual way, my mom quietly asked, "So how are you?"

My face grew hot.

I couldn't breathe.

I swallowed hard, desperately trying to maintain control and suppress the emotions that were rapidly welling inside me. And then it happened. I crumbled. Openly and unashamedly, the wounded child I had been and the restored woman I had become began to quietly cry years of tears.

After a few uncomfortable moments my mom apologetically asked, "Am I upsetting you?"

At first I couldn't speak, tears were the only thing that would come. Looking into her concerned, apprehensive eyes I softly replied, "Not at all."

Then she thanked me for seeing her, and confessed that she feared I wouldn't. After another short silence, still unsure of what to say, I finally blurted out, "It's been a long journey, and I've had to rely on God a lot. I'm serving Him now."

With that expression I was able to collect myself, feeling surefooted again about the person I was today. I dabbed my eyes with a tissue and looked at Joe, wondering what to say next. But the next words were not mine to share. Instead, my mom's eyes filled with tears and she said, "Michelle, there's something I need to do. I need to apologize for all I've done that caused you pain."

In that instant there was nothing that could have anchored me to my chair. Immediately I jumped to my feet and moved around the table to wrap my arms around my mom. And with my head on her shoulder and her arms around my neck we cried together in a moment of incredible mercy and forgiveness. I had always held my life story close, mostly to protect myself. But I realized as our tears soaked the other's shoulder, that my story became one of triumph and liberty the moment I held her. It was an indescribable moment God orchestrated to set a child free from painful memories and a mother from haunting mistakes.

When I sat back down, there was a lightness I had never felt before. Not like the happiness I felt with my husband and kids, but a lightness, as if a weight had been lifted from my shoulders. Through all God had done in my life, I believed I had been freed from all the heaviness of my past. But that day I realized that emotional and spiritual rescue, true freedom of heart and mind, can only come when we release the effects of the offense into the hands of the Healer.

For the next half hour our conversation continued with my mom offering complete transparency. She told me to ask anything. So I proceeded to ask many things, including details about my father. As anticipated, my mom could not say with certainty who he was. If it was the man she predicted, he did not reciprocate her feelings and wanted nothing to do with a child. Finally it was confirmed, no one was at the hospital when I was born.

No proud father.

No doting grandparents.

Just her and me.

As my mother shared the details, I saw the sadness of that rejection in her face. For the first time I understood it was not just me who had experienced abandonment. She too had been deeply wounded, and over the years those hurts compounded to form a foundation of confusion and defeat. A foundation from which drugs seemed to be the only escape. By the miracle of God's spirit, I was suddenly seeing my mom with eyes of compassion. We were two wounded women. One rescued by grace, the other in pursuit.

Emotionally drained, we wrapped up the conversation and went outside to the corner park where we took pictures together. As we put our arms around each other and smiled, I was struck by the fact that my mom was dressed up. A long skirt, pretty blouse, earrings, styled hair. I hadn't noticed it earlier, probably because of the nerves and apprehension. But now when I looked at her I could clearly see the time and care she had put into preparing for our meeting. She had planned on asking for my forgiveness and wanted me to see her worthy of that gift. I was moved. For all the times in my life it seemed she didn't care, this was the greatest demonstration that she did.

Not wanting the afternoon to end I suggested we visit an antique shop a few doors down. As we neared the entrance I asked if she'd ever been in the store before. And her response saddened me. She said, "No. I haven't been very many places at all. Not very many places at all."

It was heart wrenching. Her existence had been restricted by bad choices and confined by addictions, so that she never had an opportunity to enjoy her life. Once again I was moved with emotion, fully aware of the brokenness that had influenced her path.

As we weaved between the display tables I found myself speaking words of truth over my mom. I expressed how proud I was of her sobriety, and how she had been blessed with a new beginning and a new start. And as I turned the corner I caught a glimpse of a sign that summed up my wish for her; a sign I would take to the register and buy so she could have a remembrance of the day and the forgiveness we both experienced. It simply said: *Faith. Love. Jesus.*

I handed it to her with another affirmation of my confidence that she was going to make it. She held onto the sign like it was one of the most priceless treasures in the room. And indeed it was. Because I had passed along the answer I'd found and allowed her to hold that hope in her hands.

With the day growing late, we decided to go our separate ways, but planned to meet the following day at my grandparents' house for dinner. I had a difficult time sleeping that night, with the events of the day replaying in my head. I thought about the vulnerability my mom had shown sitting across from me. I knew firsthand what vulnerability felt like, and I knew it wasn't easy. I thought about the courage it took for her to express her failures and request my forgiveness. I thought about the strength it would take to leave her former life behind and pursue sobriety. And I was proud of her determination to go all in.

All in.

My eyes flew open as my heart came under immediate conviction. In order to continue the work God had begun, He needed me to go *all in* as well. Knowing exactly what that meant I nudged Joe to reveal a surprising change of heart. A decision I knew God was asking me to trust Him with.

I needed to let my mom meet my kids.

The following evening my children were introduced to their grandma. Throughout the visit she played sweetly with them and seemed very natural at being doting and attentive. She also looked comfortably maternal while holding my daughter and feeding her a bottle. Quite honestly, as I watched her relax into the situation, I envied her spirit. There seemed to be such a simplicity in it all. She had been forgiven, and was ready and willing to experience the rewards of that freedom. I couldn't decide if the years of addiction and its effects left her mind unable to distinguish the complexities that should have accompanied the situation, or if I was truly witnessing the unreserved acceptance of God's grace and mercy. But if it was the latter, it was without question the purest expression of faith I had ever witnessed.

Although I was happy to see my mom engaging with my kids, there was also a momentary pause when I wondered why she couldn't have done that with me. It was certainly a natural reaction; one that anyone with my past would experience. But as I looked at her sitting on the floor with my son, I realized this was God's miraculous supplement to forgiveness.

It was called restoration.

The gift of allowing her to express nurturing as it was intended, and the opportunity to experience important, meaningful moments that had been lost in her past. With that momentary resentment behind me, I breathed a silent prayer of thanks. As God had done in my own life, He was now preparing and orchestrating complete healing and rebirth for my mom. And that was more than I could have ever hoped or imagined.

Since our visit I have called my mom on the 15th of each month to encourage her in her journey to sobriety. We talk frequently and have been building a relationship of genuine respect and care for each other. Even more important, I sense God's continuing work in my mom's heart to establish her worth and value beyond her past. Every day I am so thankful to know that He outdoes Himself not only for me, but now for my mom as well.

On the day I met with my mom at the café, I posted this picture and message on Facebook:

Over the years a lot of healing has come from telling my story! Today is no different. I sat with my 57-year-old mom that I haven't seen in over 10 years or spoken to in eight. We talked for hours about painful things, both willing to be brave and vulnerable.
Today my mom cried as she asked for forgiveness for all the decisions she made in her life that caused me so much pain. I held her in my arms, and the past that had always seemed so close was suddenly far away! Today I forgave my mom... Today I am proud of my mom's sobriety... Today I gained a new perspective on healing... Today I thank Jesus for rescuing me and the life He's given me!

At the end of the post I referenced the name of the café. Several days later a friend contacted me regarding the message. She had followed the link to the café's Facebook page, and during her perusal found a picture of the storefront. The photo revealed the red-brick building with the green and white striped awning. But it was the banner above the awning that caught her attention and excited her.

It read: *With God, all things are possible.*

Chills ran up and down my spine as my eyes filled with tears. In that moment I understood that God had appointed that location, and ordained that very moment in time to accomplish something transforming. With God, the very thing my scarred heart for years considered impossible, was miraculously moved into the realm of reality. With God, forgiveness was given, healing occurred, the past was redeemed, and the future was rewritten. With God, it was all possible, and He did it out of His incredible love for me. With that realization, I stepped into another significant level of healing. Not only had I been reunited with my mom, but my heart had finally found a father, in my God.

An exclamation point is used to indicate strong feelings, and often marks the end of a sentence. As powerful as this chapter has been to my story, it by no means marks the end. The one thing I've learned for certainty about my God, is that He's not done yet. When I look back, I thought forgiveness would be the highlight of my life. But then came incredible growth and purpose. When I thought marriage was the ultimate expression of love, then came my beautiful children. When I thought there could be no greater blessing than my family, then came total healing and restoration of my heart.

At every turn God has outdone Himself for me, blessing me beyond my wildest dreams. I didn't deserve it. I didn't earn it. But thankfully, it's not about me. It's about God in me. His desire to fill my life with His love and promises and purpose. And for the remainder of my life, I am confident I will be the blessed recipient of many amazing exclamation points.

I will close by saying, *I cannot wait!* And I pray that you, too, will discover all the ways God wants to outdo Himself for you.

Reconnected

PART VI

Meant To Be Known

In Isaiah 55:9, God declares that His ways are higher than our ways, and His thoughts higher than our thoughts. In His wisdom reconciliation was meant to be part of my story; its significance and purpose was fully known in just two short years.

At the end of June 2017, I received a phone call from my mom. I had still been making my monthly calls celebrating her continued sobriety, but this time was random – her reaching out to me. During the call she expressed great sorrow over losing her mother just four months prior. I had seen my maternal grandmother only once when I was very young. The addictions my mom battled all her life were habits they had in common. Hand-me-down brokenness, if you will.

Maybe the loss hit her so hard because it made her keenly aware of the mother-daughter bond. With tears she expressed her happiness about the recent reconciliation with my younger sister. Her voice broke as she counted herself blessed to be in communication with her daughters again. Her heart's confession reminded me of the vulnerability she showed at our café meeting almost two years earlier.

Sadly, that was the last time I would ever talk with my mom.

On July 6, 2017 at 8:30 p.m., I received a phone call informing me that my mom had been found by her husband – she was not breathing. After being revived by paramedics she was taken to the hospital and listed in critical condition. Wanting to assess the situation so I could decide my course of action, I called the hospital and talked to the ICU nurse. He explained the situation was not good, and his recommendation would be to gather the family.

I was on a red-eye flight to Illinois in a matter of hours. All I could do on the flight was pray that God would allow me to talk with my mom, but when I arrived at the hospital I found her heavily sedated. The doctors explained that prior to the paramedic's revival efforts, she lost oxygen to the brain. They didn't know for how long, but the lack appeared to have caused significant damage.

The nurses encouraged us to keep trying to communicate with her, but cautioned us to not expect a response. For the next six days I rarely left my mom's side. I wanted to be there to talk to her, and sing and read scriptures. I painted her fingernails, all the while speaking to her about her beauty and worth. And in a moment when sheer exhaustion took over, I even danced a silly little dance for my mom. She never responded, and may never have been aware of my moment of spontaneity, but that was okay, because for the first time I felt like a little girl free to be myself with my mom.

Thoroughly exhausted from the vigil, a family friend asked why I didn't go get a few hours of rest and come back to the hospital the next morning. My answer was immediate and revealed the total forgiveness my heart had experienced over the past two years. In my life I knew too well what it was like to be left alone and vulnerable, and I didn't want that for my mom. If she woke, I wanted to be there. It was my desire to share a piece of the beautiful gift God gave me when He surrounded me with people that loved me when I needed it most.

As I kept watch I was amazed to hear who my mom had become over the years. People stopping by to visit recounted how Laura (my mom) was always willing to help when someone was in need. A relative shared that she had been a great support when his wife became ill, another visitor told of how she helped pregnant girls and women coming out of rehabilitation, and finally the account of how she cared three months for her dying mother.

It was a beautiful revelation for me to see my mom from a new perspective, and to hear what a giving spirit she had. As people shared I realized that long before our reconciliation God had begun to bring her gifts and goodness, once overshadowed by brokenness, into the light. It was a beautiful confirmation that He had been writing both of our stories at the same time. She was changing and growing while I was changing and growing – both of us being prepared for the closing chapter God intended.

With no response in six days, my mom's husband made the decision to remove her from all life support. I broke down when the papers were signed. Thankfully my younger sister made it in time to see my mom before support was removed. By God's grace and favor we were able to arrange a phone call from my brother in prison. We held the phone to my mom's ear as he expressed his sadness for the situation.

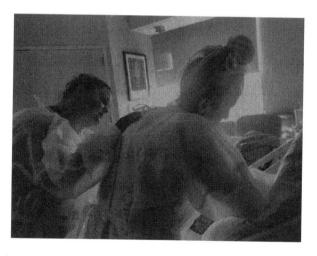

My sister Kathy and me by our Mom's bedside.

Soon after the doctors took my mom off of the support and sedatives, she opened her eyes. But there was no connection with anyone in the room, and no response to noise stimulus. There was simply a far-away stare, accompanied by an occasional groan.

The groaning continued for two days. I asked the doctor if she was in pain, but since she wasn't communicating, he couldn't offer a definitive answer. Determined to be her advocate, I called Joe's family and asked them to come pray over my mom. Soon we stood around her bed reading scripture and inviting peace into her room, and with our voices raised in agreement, my mom finally grew silent and calm.

As the hours ticked away, I continued to stroke my mom's hair and hold her hand. I sang to her, spoke words of comfort and promise, and thanked her for the gift of reconciliation. One of the final things I whispered was that she would soon be running into the welcoming arms of Jesus, and that He would give her an amazing crown – one that I would recognize her by when I joined her in heaven.

Within days of that declaration, my mom passed peacefully into her eternity.

As I contemplated the two years preceding her home-going, I was filled with awe at the wonders of God's grace. In His plan, my mom was always meant to be known as a loving mother, and a mother who was loved. Through her surrender to God's relentless pursuit of her heart, and His amazing gift of forgiveness, she received and experienced that honor.

In His plan, I was always meant to be known as a daughter who was loved, as well as a loving daughter.

Through my surrender to God's relentless desire to restore, and His amazing gift of healing and reconciliation, I received and experienced that blessing.

In each case, response was the key. My mom had to respond to the Spirit's plea to stop running from her Healer. She had to respond when He asked her to seek my forgiveness. And I had to respond with mercy and compassion when my Healer said *it is time.*

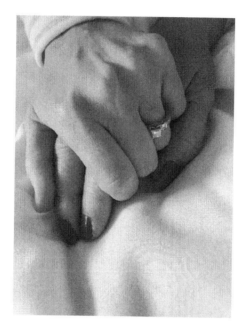

Only the God of timing could have orchestrated the most beautiful chapter of my mom's life story – a chapter in which I was privileged to be a part. And with that beautiful ending, my mom found the peace she had always needed, and my heart was gifted with the liberty and wholeness I had always longed for.

Through this wonderful, amazing journey, I have learned that His ways are truly above our ways, and am convinced that by giving Him our lives and trust, each one of us can be known as rescued, restored, and deeply loved. As you continue to walk through your story, my wholehearted encouragement is – pursue to be known. Discover His best, and live amazed in His grace.

Acknowledgements

To my Joe Joe, Cohen Boy, and Sweet Annalee...You are my life, my joy and have made me the richest woman. Thank you for the adventure of our amazing life!

To my Mom...Thank you for showing me that true healing and forgiveness are possible.

To my Grandparents...Thank you for taking a chance on a little girl that didn't have much to offer. You knew if you told me about Jesus my life would never be the same. For this I am forever grateful! Love you!

To Bill, Glenda, Jeremy, Justin, Amber, Jon, Joelyn, Dave & Callie...the family that gave me the gift of a last name! When Joe proposed he said that I would become a part of a family and heritage founded on faith and love. I still can't believe I have a new mom, dad, brudder's, sisters, nieces and nephew to love and learn from. What a beautiful gift the RABY name is. We now get to pass it along to our children as their inheritance.

To David, Lynda, Kate and David Austin...Thank you for adopting me into your family. Throughout the years, you have not only supported my dreams, but have been the biggest encouragers. When I didn't believe, you believed for me and when I wanted to give up you taught me how to press on. Your consistency and unconditional love has led me to a new found confidence in myself. I'm honored to call you family!

To the Pastors and my Capital Christian Center Family...Thank you for providing a safe place for me to heal. It started as a hiding place, but grew into so much more. It's the place where my faith was built and I recognized the faithful hand of God in my life. It's the where I met JoeJoe at the altar on our wedding day. It's where I watched our babies lift their hands in worship. It's where I found safe friendships that will last a lifetime. Because of this I know without a doubt that He's always working and will always be with me.

To everyone else in my life from Salem, Olney and Edwardsville...So many of you opened your doors and hearts to care for a girl right where she was without judgement. You will never know how your unconditional love has changed my life and helped make me into the woman I am today.

Many years ago this book was a dream and became a reality when Renee Davis said YES to God. This turned into a five year journey with countless coffee dates, stopping the process, and starting again because God wasn't finished with the story.

This dream wouldn't have been possible if it weren't for countless people that I get to do life with. In various ways they are a part of this book. Thank you Joe, Trent, Sarah, Christa, Renee Ross & Staci for your part in making this book a reality.

About the Authors

Michelle Raby – Growing up, Michelle didn't know who her father was, she never had one. In the first decade of her life, she lived in a home that ran off of drugs and alcohol, suffered from many forms of abuse, was held at gunpoint, and her siblings died in an accident. She was not destined for success, but thankfully, the plans for her life were bigger than she could have ever imagined. 20 years later, she is living a life that is beyond her wildest dreams. She's the Outreach Director at Capital Christian Center in Sacramento, California, a long way from her hometown in Southern Illinois. She's been involved with numerous outreaches and spearheaded several initiatives reaching out to the local homeless, youth, and special needs communities with different events year round. She credits her passion for the marginalized and voiceless in our world to the journey she has been brought through.

Her journey has also brought her the most cherished possession- a last name. When her husband, Joe, proposed, he said he wanted to give her the gift of a last name. They've continued that name with their two amazing children, Cohen and Annalee. And even though she still doesn't know who her dad is, She knows who her FATHER is –

a gracious and redeeming God who has restored her and given her hope.

R M Davis – At this writing Renee Davis lives in Gold River, CA. She received a Ministerial Arts Degree from Trinity School of the Bible in Sacramento. She is a screenwriter and children's book author, offering hope and inspiration to journeyers of all ages. For more on her work visit www.whimspiration.com

My Amazing Life!

Me and My Joe Joe

Our Family of 4

Processed with Rookie Cam

Our Cohen Boy and Sweet Annalee

My Girls

The family that gave me the gift of a last name!!

Made in the USA
San Bernardino, CA
18 January 2018